LONE VOYAGER

LONE
VOYAGER

One Woman's Journey of
Self-Discovery

MAUREEN JENKINS

PIATKUS

Published in the UK in 2000 by
Judy Piatkus (Publishers) Limited
5 Windmill Street
London W1P 1HF
e-mail: info@piatkus.co.uk

For the latest news and information on all our titles
visit our website at **www.piatkus.co.uk**

The moral rights of the author have been asserted

A catalogue record for this book is available from the British Library

ISBN 0 7499 2018 1

Designed by Random
Edited by Esther Jagger

Set by Phoenix Photosetting, Chatham, Kent
Printed and bound in Great Britain by
Mackays of Chatham plc, Chatham, Kent

FOR PAUL

My special, heartfelt thanks to Paul Fay,
without whose love and support my path
would not have been so smooth

One ship sails east and another west
By the selfsame winds that blow
'Tis the set of the sail
And not the gale
That determines the way they go.

Like the winds of the sea are the ways
of fate
As we journey along through life.
'Tis the set of the soul
That decides the goal,
And not the calm or the strife.

Anon.

CONTENTS

ACKNOWLEDGEMENTS

I would like to express my sincere gratitude to Paul Fay, Philip Rose, my sons Russel and Colin, my parents Reg and Jean, my sisters Sheila and Valerie, my dearest friend Jo Bennett, and finally to so many of my new-found friends, especially Rodney Cattell. Their love, encouragement and help were my guiding stars for the course I chose to steer.

I am indebted to all the members of the Joshua Slocum Society International for their generosity and the hospitality extended to me during the centenary celebrations. I would also like to thank the many people I have met in America whose love and friendship I will carry with me wherever I venture.

Although I have been able to mention by name many of the wonderful people I encountered during my voyages, those whom I have not named are just as important. You know who you are – you may not appear in this book, but you are imprinted on my heart. Thank you for your warmth, kindness and hospitality; one day I hope our paths will cross again.

CHAPTER ONE

DAWNING OF A DREAM

I was desperately trying to get some rest despite the worst weather conditions I had ever experienced. Suddenly, at 3a.m. I was shocked from my fragile peace by a dreadful sound like a tremendous crack of thunder overhead. *Lucia* immediately picked up speed – too much speed. I leapt from my bunk in the main cabin, switched on the deck lights and staggered out into the cockpit. The noise from the wind screaming through the rigging was deafening. The pounding of the huge seas against *Lucia*'s hull sounded like Neptune was walloping her. I could see that the forward headsail had started to unfurl a little from the top, but that did not seem too big a problem – all I had to do was refurl it. Naïveté is a wonderful thing.

The weather was turning into a full-blown gale and we were dashing along at a dangerous speed – between six to seven knots. I knew I had to slow *Lucia* down, so I dropped the reefed mainsail and tried to refurl the headsail – but it refused to respond to my efforts. I just could not understand why.

I put on my safety harness and crawled along the side

1

deck to get a better view. But the mast lights only shone from the first set of spreaders down, leaving the upper part of the mast in darkness and making it impossible to see the top of the unfurled sail. The spray from the mountainous sea was blinding me, so I clawed my way back to the safety of the cockpit. *Lucia* and I were being shaken like rag dolls, and the combination of violent motion and fear had got my stomach in a stranglehold. This was the last thing I needed – I was furious that my seasickness had returned with such a vengeance.

Yet I knew I had to do something to take the pressure off the rig. So after a short while I cautiously made my way forward again. But still the lack of light and sheets of spray whipping from the enormous waves made it impossible to see, and I returned to the cockpit once more to await the dawn. All too soon my stomach reacted and I had to pay homage to Neptune again.

When the first rays of daylight appeared, I went forward to reassess the problem. Somehow the wind had managed to tease open about one third of the sail from the top, which made it act like a balloon with an uncontrollable thrust of power. The pressure had caused it to jam solid. No matter what I did, it would not budge. I went to the mast and tried to lower the sail, but because the sheet was so tightly wound around it, I only managed to bring it down by six inches. At the time I felt it helped a little, but in reality the only thing it helped was my state of mind. I returned to the cockpit wet, exhausted and feeling very sick.

I went below, lay down in my bunk and tried to do some serious thinking. I just had to come up with a way of solving this problem. I had fought long and hard to bring my dream to fruition, and I was determined not to fall at the first hurdle.

What must have been another line squall hit *Lucia* again, and I lay there wondering what might happen next. Were we going to be knocked down? Was *Lucia* going to turn over? I cast my eyes around the cabin. Had I stowed everything securely? Or was some apparently innocuous item going to turn into a dangerous missile?

I started to hear a sound like a jet engine roaring towards us, and then for a second or two there was complete silence. The wave that engulfed *Lucia* must have been enormous. The sea rushed through the dorade ventilators and poured into the cabin as if someone had turned on a dozen fire hydrants. As I was lying directly under one of them, I took the full force of the Atlantic in my face! I shot up, shut all the vents and laid towels over the cabin sole to mop up the water. I lay down on my soggy bunk again and tried to see the funny side. What a pickle to get into – my beautiful dry cabin awash with seawater, all through my inexperience. Next time I would make sure the vents were closed before the weather deteriorated.

By 8a.m. I was very anxious to talk to Paul on the radio. Having built *Lucia* and taught me how to sail her, he knew us both extremely well; I felt hopeful that he would come up with a solution. I called him several times on the prearranged frequency, but to no avail. On the one morning I really needed him for something other than a friendly chat he wasn't there! I changed frequencies and called up the British Maritime Net; Bruce, the net operator, allowed me to call Paul the moment he heard I had a problem. Again, no response; I called and called, there was just no answer. Bruce and another guy on the net were both experienced sailors and told me not to worry about contacting Paul, as they could help me. But the only suggestion they could offer, that I had not already tried, was to wrap my spare halyard around the balloon in the sail and pull it as tight as I could, so that the wind could not fill it.

Sitting in the relative safety of *Lucia*'s cabin, my dread of going on deck again conflicted with my anxiety to solve the problem. The latter won. So, feeling very weak, I went out into the cockpit, clipped on my safety harness and carefully made my way up to the bows. The seas were unbelievably wild and fear-inspiring. Wedging myself against the guardrail, I took hold of the spare halyard and tried to get it around the sail. After repeated attempts I managed to do so once, but with the wind whipping at the halyard it was impossible to do the job effectively.

The conditions had not improved since my 3a.m. alarm call. With the terrifying noise of the wind screaming in the rigging and my eyes stinging and sightless from spray off the twenty-foot-high waves, I quickly decided this was no place for a human being. I secured the halyard, dropped down on all fours and crawled back along the side deck into the relative calm of the cabin.

Back at the radio I reported to the net again. Once more I tried to call Paul, but still there was no response. Then Bruce asked me to stand by as his telephone was ringing. He seemed to be gone a long time, but when he returned, joy of joys, he told me it was Paul on the line. Within seconds I heard the wonderful sound of his voice come over the air.

He had heard me call him at 0800 hours, but his radio would not transmit – frustratingly, he had heard every word but was unable to respond. He had then driven to a fellow radio ham's house two miles away and asked him to tune into the correct frequency, while he called Bruce on the telephone. After going over all the possible solutions with me, Paul agreed that in my weakened state the best thing I could do was head for the nearest harbour, La Coruna in northern Spain.

'But the first thing I want you to do is lie down in

your bunk and get some rest,' he ordered. '*Lucia*'s an extremely strong boat – don't worry about her, she'll take care of herself. But *you* must get some rest, and then maybe the seasickness will abate.'

Feeling cold and weak, but a great deal more at peace now that I had made contact with Paul, I took his advice. Exhaustion took hold of my body and I did sleep for a while, but it was not long before *Lucia's* motion broke through my dreams and brought me back to harsh reality. I changed course and headed towards La Coruna, feeling extremely disappointed that my first landfall was only going to be Spain and not, as intended, the Azores. But I was determined: God willing the Azores would be next!

That night, sleepless and queasy as I endured the dreadful vibrating motion of *Lucia*, I thought back to how it had all started – to the moment when I first realised my life was at last going to move off in a new direction. The change came about by pure chance. In 1989, my husband and I were on holiday in Fowey, Cornwall. He had been trying to hire a sailing boat, but owing to our complete lack of experience no one would let him have one. The only thing he was able to arrange was an hour's tuition on a sailing dinghy. This did not appeal to me at all but, as always, he persuaded me to do what he wanted.

My reluctance made it difficult for me to pay attention to the instructor during the pre-sail class. Once aboard the dinghy, I sat gripping the jib sheet, my knuckles white with fear, as my husband propelled the dinghy forward at an alarming speed and angle. When the instructor told us to swap places and I took my turn at the helm, I was sure I would be pitched overboard in seconds. However, as I carefully followed the tutor's instructions, I realised that I was able to control what happened, and as my fear lifted my confidence began to grow.

LONE VOYAGER

By the end of that first lesson I had become completely enthralled. The thrill of dashing along on the surface of the water and tacking the dinghy through the wind was intoxicating. I pleaded with the instructor to squeeze me in for some more lessons. Over the next three days, with just four hours of tuition I had been bitten so hard by the sailing bug that I just could not restrain my joy. My husband, on the other hand, didn't enjoy sailing at all. Little did he realise the road he had unwittingly started me on.

When I got back from holiday, with the support of my two grown-up sons, I started to look for a small yacht on which I could learn to sail properly. I was very lucky to find *MacNab*, a rather ancient twenty-seven foot fibre glass yacht known as a MacWester. Although I felt my husband would never willingly have allowed me to purchase a yacht, after a great deal of persuasion by myself and my sons, he finally gave me permission to buy her. I devoted every spare moment to my new acquisition. On the first day we took her out of the harbour, even though I had only a vague idea of what to do. I loved every minute of it.

That day in the harbour there was the most beautiful yacht I had ever seen, strong and elegant like a superb black swan. We circled her in *MacNab* before returning to our mooring, and once we were back I could not take my eyes off her. There was something about the shape of *Kocum*'s hull that instilled confidence, and I felt inexplicably drawn to her. I asked the harbour master about her, and my eagerness must have been transparent because later that day he arranged for my husband and me to meet the skipper and his wife. When Sheila and Graham invited us on board and I looked over *Kocum* a dream began to form deep within me.

It seemed crazy at the time, but I instinctively knew where my future lay. One day I would have a yacht like

Kocum. I would live aboard alone and sail her single-handed wherever I wanted to go. But for the time being I knew I would have to keep these longings to myself; I would have to be content with *MacNab* and, more to the point, use her to learn how to sail.

If I was ever going to transform my dream into reality, I realised there were many other hurdles ahead of me. My life had always been complicated, mainly due to my desire never to hurt other people's feelings. To the outside world I appeared to be a successful businesswoman, with a fulfilled personal life as a wife and mother of two grown-up sons. Yet throughout my marriage I had become very skilled at hiding my true feelings; in fact I had been desperately unhappy for many years.

I got married at the age of twenty, in October 1966, to a young man who I knew was not right for me. But, since I was pregnant with our first child, I was hopeful that I could make the marriage work. Although my new husband was full of fun and seemed to be very popular, I was soon to realise that he had another, darker side to his personality. I also had a dreadful secret that I could not share with him, and which was to remain locked away guiltily inside me for many years.

Since my husband was a year younger than me, to begin with I made excuses for his moods and unpredictable behaviour. I put it down to his youth, telling myself that one day he would mature and that, if I really tried hard, maybe we could make a go of it.

Colin was born on 6 April 1967, after a long and difficult labour. I adored my new baby and experienced great joy in motherhood, but unfortunately my husband grew terribly jealous. I had a tiny, helpless baby who really needed my attention, yet I had to ensure that I did not obviously give him more time and attention than I did my husband.

Nine months after Colin was born I was pregnant

again, and I felt sure my husband would not be happy about it. However, his response caught me completely by surprise. 'Kids are great,' he stated. 'We should have lots of them!'

Russel was born on 1 October 1968 at home. My mother came to stay and look after Colin until I was strong enough to cope again. The day after Russel's birth my husband left the house at 10a.m., saying he would be back in a couple of hours. When he still had not returned by two the following morning my mother grew quite distraught. I had to explain to her that this was by no means unusual, which led to her asking more questions than I was prepared to answer. When it was time for her to return home she pleaded with me to take the children and come with her. However, I did not think this was the answer to my problems. I promised her that I would be fine, and did my best to allay her worries.

Although all my waking hours were fully occupied with bringing up the boys and helping my husband run our antiques business, my by now very unhappy marriage weighed heavily on me. I was working hard in the business and I felt that I was getting very little help from him with the boys or with any domestic chores, and as a result I was always tired.

I was under tremendous strain. At one point I had a minor breakdown. I remember very little about it, but my husband told me that he had found me in bed one night, acting like a zombie. He said he had put hot and cold items into my hands to try to elicit some sort of response, but to no avail. It was only during the early hours of the morning when Russel began to cry that I came out of my stupor and got up to see to him. Later that day my husband took me to the doctor, who diagnosed me as being under severe stress and said that my mind had just switched off.

It was obvious to me that I could not continue putting up with this terrible domestic situation. For one thing, the boys would soon be old enough to be aware of what was going on. But whenever I mentioned my feeling that we would be better off living apart, my husband would disagree. I felt trapped in this difficult and troubled relationship.

Slowly I began to learn how to deal with his behaviour. Much against my will, I made myself placate him instead of doing things that from experience I knew would arouse his anger. He actually became quite happy with me, and would often tell me I was a 'good girl'. As I became more adept at judging his mood, life seemed to settle down. He was away from home a great deal of the time, travelling the country to buy stock, and for this I was very grateful.

Despite the long hours put in by both of us, in the early years money was in very short supply. I therefore worked not only in the business but also outside it to supplement our income. When the children were very small I was able to take them with me to the shop, and in the evenings I hired a baby sitter and set up 'house parties' at which I sold reproduction copper and brass ornaments to groups of people.

As the years passed we changed tack from antiques and started up a business buying and selling commercial vehicles. Then we progressed to renting out the vehicles. By now the boys were at secondary school, and at the age of thirty-two I felt strong enough to broach once more the subject of living away from my husband.

It seemed to me that he would be pleased to be relieved of us as a family. I had thought long and hard about the best way of approaching the subject of separation. I felt confident that if I just talked to him quietly and sensibly he would see that all our lives would be enhanced if the boys and I lived apart from him.

But I could not have been more wrong: his response was far worse than I had imagined. Some hours later I was convinced that he meant everything he said and I was in no doubt that if I left him, I would not set eyes on the boys again. Surely, I told myself, it would be better to return to my previous strategy and bide my time until Colin and Russel were older.

Although the boys appeared to be asleep during this dreadful episode, I was concerned that they might have heard more than was good for them. In my desperate frame of mind I resolved to make all our lives as free from conflict as I could. I seemed to be successful in my endeavours, because no one in our vicinity showed any signs of being aware of my inner despair. I managed to keep myself going by building on the conviction that I had nursed since the early days of my marriage, that one day I would have my freedom.

Life continued, as I put everything I had into bringing up the boys and making the business as successful as possible. Having survived the recession of 1979, the company went from strength to strength. My role was to deal with the administrative and financial side.

By now the boys were at the point of leaving school. Colin, who was bright, took A-levels and then went to University College London to do a biology degree. Between getting his A-levels and going to UCL he took a year off and went travelling with friends in India. Russel was less academic by nature and chose to study art at college, but after one year he decided it was not for him and joined us in the business. But this too proved unsuccessful and eventually he left. At nineteen he was diagnosed manic-depressive and spent some time in hospital, after which I nursed him at home. In due course, he became stable enough to cope without my help, and at that point he moved into his own independent accommodation.

With the boys gone I spent a lot of time on my own. Once the working day was over my husband would go to the pub, not returning home until late in the evening. Then he would simply eat his meal and fall asleep.

But being on my own was no problem as far as I was concerned, and in the early 1990s I spent as much time as I could aboard my delightful new acquisition *MacNab*. The sense of peace and well being I felt there was wonderful. My husband had decided that he passionately loathed both *MacNab* and sailing, so I explained to him repeatedly that he need not be involved. I did not expect him to do something he did not care for, I told him, and was more than happy to go sailing with our sons or friends. But that was not what he wanted either, and he kept trying to stop me going to the boat. It became increasingly difficult to go sailing, but by now my dream had taken such a hold on me that, no matter what the consequences, I went.

I arranged one day for an instructor to take Russel and me on a RYA (Royal Yacht Association) Competent Crew Course. Michael Parker arrived to look *MacNab* over and agreed that, despite her age, she was fit to go to sea. We planned a three-day trip from Watermouth harbour in North Devon to Tenby in South Wales, via Appledore and Lundy Island.

I remember that experience very well. We had great difficulty leaving the mooring, due to the low equinoctial tides. When we did finally manage to leave Watermouth and head towards Appledore the sky darkened and we were engulfed by an electrical storm. Within minutes visibility was reduced to a few feet, and we crossed the notorious Bideford Bar with our hearts in our mouths. We followed the buoys marked on the chart, but once we had passed the last one, we ran aground in the river at Appledore on a falling tide.

When we dried out, *MacNab*'s bows were pointing

towards the sky in a most unseaman-like fashion. During the early hours of the next morning, when we were afloat once more, a fishing boat came past and advised us to pick up a mooring close to the lifeboat.

'If you stay where you are, you'll be aground in a few hours,' said the skipper.

We didn't like to tell him that was how we had got there in the first place!

The whole trip was beset by bad weather and instead of being out for three days, we were away for seven. When we got back to Watermouth my husband met us. He obviously expected the trip to have got sailing out of my system, and he could not understand why I had such a big smile on my face.

'It was terrific! We've had an amazing time and I feel we've learnt so much more than if the weather had been fair,' I bubbled.

Russel and I received our certificates for Competent Crew and I got an extra one for Day Skipper. Keeping up the momentum, I enrolled at the North Devon College in Barnstaple, for evening classes in the first of the shore-based courses on navigation.

Now that both boys had left home I felt it was time to do something positive about my own situation. I presented my husband with a *fait accompli*; I would continue to work at the company full time, but I had to be allowed to live away from him for a short time, to see if I could work things out. I moved into a flat very close to the North Devon Yacht Club, overlooking the estuary at Instow. Slowly the feelings of desperation I had endured for so long began to lift. As each day passed, no matter how difficult it was to work with my husband, when I returned to the flat I had time to think and plan for my future. I joined the yacht club and, although it took a lot of courage to step through the door that first night, I was so very glad I did.

One of the tutors from my navigation class, Philip Rose, was there and I got into conversation with him. I told him how keen I was to go sailing as crew and asked him advice as to how I should go about it.

'Well,' he offered, 'if you're free in the morning you can crew for me. It will be an early start, mind – you'll have to be here just before seven.'

'That's wonderful,' I enthused. 'Where are you planning to go?'

'Clovelly. We'll be away all day, returning on the evening tide.'

We had a marvellous time the next day. For me sailing held a magic that is difficult to describe; somehow it washed my soul clean of even the most problematic aspects of my life. I learnt a great deal from Philip and enjoyed his company immensely. Now in his mid-sixties, he had led a very varied life. When he was younger he had been an actor and could still spin a yarn in such a way to keep me spellbound. During World War II he had been a signalman in the Navy and he had a great respect and love of the sea, although, like me, he had not come to sailing until relatively late in life. Over the next few months I crewed for Philip many times. I soon became aware that he was a very wise and knowledgeable person, a man for whom I have tremendous respect. We became firm friends.

After four months of my husband's constant pleading and promises that life would be completely different if I returned, I weakened and said I would give it one more try. But within two weeks I knew I had made a mistake. As far as he was concerned he was very happy and just wanted the marriage to continue in the same manner. I knew without a shadow of doubt that I would have to end it.

Shortly after my return to the family home, Philip asked me if I would crew for him on a trip to Roscoff in

Brittany, Bideford's twin town. A French yacht was planning to leave on the same day for Bideford. Both vessels would carry gifts and information about their respective towns. I jumped at this chance: a forty-eight-hour trip across the English Channel would be a wonderful learning opportunity for me. But during the voyage the weather was far from kind and I was seasick for most of the trip, though it did not stop me doing my watch or anything else that was asked of me. At one point Philip said, 'You have the look of a long-distance sailor about you.' I could hardly believe my ears – it was as if he could read my mind. I decided to confide in him and told him that I wanted to own a yacht like *Kocum*, a steel 'Spray', live aboard and sail single-handed to those parts of the world that I wanted to visit.

Philip started to tell me a little about the *Spray* and her famous Canadian captain, Joshua Slocum, who in 1895–8 was the first man to sail single-handed around the world. I decided I wanted to find out more about this extraordinary man. Then we began to discuss my dream in depth, and I was amazed at his confidence in my determination and ability to bring my dream to fruition. He advised me to seek the help of a man called Paul Fay, who by coincidence was doing some work on *MacNab* for me.

As we approached Roscoff I began to feel a little better. We were met by a launch carrying local French dignitaries who were delighted to see us. The French crew had decided not to set sail, as they felt the weather was not fit for a small craft to cross the English Channel. What is it they say about 'Mad dogs and Englishmen'? Again, due to bad weather my learning curve was steep.

On account of the deteriorating weather even we mad sea-dogs were unable to sail back to the UK on Philip's yacht, but had to take the ferry to Plymouth. My husband met us, and on the drive back to North Devon he appeared irritated every time Philip and I mentioned our trip. After dropping Philip off, we returned home in silence.

When we arrived our housekeeper and Russel were in the kitchen and my husband decided to return to work. Before he left I asked him that if I was asleep when he got back, he should not disturb me. That night, after he came home, I decided once and for all that my marriage was over, and I moved to a room next to my son's.

I was glad that Russel was staying at the family home for a few days. The next morning, while Russel was still in the house, I told my husband that I could not continue to live with him. I said that if he would not leave then I would find another home as soon as possible and move out for good.

After my husband had walked out of the house, Russel appeared and asked what was going on. Without going into any details of the events of the previous night, I told my son that, no matter how difficult it might prove to be, I had resolved to end my marriage. Those few days were certainly a watershed in my life.

CHAPTER TWO

MOVING ON

The next few weeks were extremely traumatic as I worked full time, tried to find a place to live and still somehow managed to keep my plans moving forward. I arranged to meet Paul Fay at the yacht club boat park, where he had been working on *MacNab*. It was pouring with rain and, as we sheltered in my car, I casually asked him if he knew of any second-hand steel Sprays that might be for sale.

'Why?'

It has to be said at this point that, although I knew Paul only slightly, he appeared to be a very serious man of few words who rarely smiled. Yet I felt sure that, if I told him what was in my mind he would fall about in fits of laughter.

'I'd just like you to keep a good look out for one, please.'

'Unless you tell me what you want one for, I'm not sure I can help you.'

I sat there in silence for a while, wondering what to tell him. He opened the car door to leave.

Hastily I said, 'I want to buy one and adapt it for single-handed sailing.' He closed the car door.

'Why?'

'I don't think you'll understand – you'll just laugh at me.'

'Try me.'

I started to tell him of my dream, but it all sounded so impossible, that I just stopped halfway through and looked at him.

'Go on,' he insisted.

When I had finished there was complete silence – no laughter, as I had feared. Maybe he can't think of any way to respond to this crazy idea, I thought.

Then he looked me straight in the eye. 'Second-hand Spray's rarely come up for sale. Why don't you build one?' he suggested.

'That's simple to answer. I haven't got the skills – and I just wouldn't know where to begin.'

'No, I understand that. But I *do* have the skills – and if you build one it will be cheaper than converting a second-hand one and you'll get exactly what you want.'

My heart began to beat faster. Not only did this man not laugh at me, but he actually appeared to be offering his own expertise to help me achieve my ambition.

'Give me a little time to think this through and come up with some costings. Let's talk about it again in a week.'

In the next few days I asked as many people as I could about Paul. Did he have the skills required? What did he know about sailing? My instincts told me I could trust him – were they right? Everyone I spoke to gave him a glowing reference. In due course Paul appeared at my office armed with costings and photographs of the boats he had previously built. Two hours later we shook hands and the deal was sealed. It was so difficult to contain my excitement – there would be no stopping me now!

As Paul and I sat looking at the photographs of Paul's first yacht, *Faizark*, I became aware that my husband was staring through the glass panel of my office door. He entered without knocking and asked what was going on. When I introduced him to Paul and explained that we were discussing the building of a yacht for me he responded in exactly the way I could have predicted, pouring scorn on the idea and ordering me straight back to work. He stood there, waiting for me to do so.

'Would you be kind enough to close the door behind you as you go?' I retorted. Knowing how easily my words might provoke my husband, I was astonished at my own bravery. I can only assume that I was fuelled by a deep desire to make it clear to him that my future plans were no concern of his. Unexpectedly, he turned and left.

Paul arranged for us to go to Swansea Marina to view two Sprays, a stretched twenty-eight footer and a thirty-three footer. I took the day off work and we set out very early, hardly noticing as the miles slipped by because we had so much to talk about. When we got there we stood at the top of the marina gazing down at row after row of beautiful yachts.

'There's the twenty-eight footer,' said Paul pointing to the right, 'and over on the left is the thirty-three footer.'

I could not believe my eyes – the thirty-three-foot yacht was *Kocum*, the Spray I had first seen in Watermouth harbour and the one I just knew I could fulfil my dream in. I stood there speechless for a moment.

'We'll go and look at the twenty-eight foot one first.'

'No need. I want you to build that one,' I replied, pointing at *Kocum*.

Ever practical, Paul advised, 'Before you make up your mind you really should look at both of them.'

But in the end there was no contest. Having looked at

the twenty-eight-foot Spray I just could not wait to go aboard *Kocum* again. Graham, her skipper, met us as we walked along the pontoon and gave me a warm welcome, and this time the guided tour went into great detail. As I slowly looked over *Kocum*'s interior, I could clearly see how her twelve-foot beam could accommodate all I required to turn my own yacht into a very comfortable home. After making a close inspection of the deck Paul pointed out how easy it would be to redesign the coachroof to give even more space inside.

Kocum's cockpit was very deep and gave me a feeling of great security. This was just as well, because when I stood behind the helm looking forward she seemed vast. I stayed there for ages wondering if I would be able to handle such a large vessel, and asked Graham lots of questions about how she performed at sea and what problems he had encountered when manoeuvring her in tight spaces. Both Graham and Paul sang the praises of the Spray's seakeeping qualities. They assured me that she would prove to be very stable in most conditions – not a racing machine but a safe vessel, ideal for ocean passages. Paul was sure that with practice I would soon learn to manoeuvre her in harbour.

They left me alone to wander around the deck, and I made mental notes of the points I wanted to discuss with Paul on the journey back to Devon. As we left I looked back at *Kocum* from the pontoon; everything about her instilled confidence in me. I turned to Paul and said:

'She's big but I'm sure she's right for me and I'll just have to learn how to handle her.'

'Give yourself a little more time to think this project over,' advised Paul. 'Then if you're really sure this is what you want to do, we'll send for a set of plans.'

We were coming up to a bank holiday weekend, and Philip and Paul were planning to sail Philip's yacht

LONE VOYAGER

Kittiwake from Plymouth around Land's End to Bideford. They asked me if I would like to join them. This was a much-needed chance to get away from my personal problems, so I happily agreed.

On the Thursday evening I was busy at home sorting out my sailing gear when my husband appeared and asked me what I was doing. I told him about the planned sailing weekend, and he insisted on me giving him an assurance that I would not go. I was unable to do this and pointed out that it was really my own business what I did over the bank holiday.

I thought that it would only make matters worse if I continued packing, so I made my excuses, claiming that I was very tired, and went to my room. Sometime later, while I was quietly finishing my packing, the door opened and in strode my husband. He appeared to be very agitated and again he tried to convince me that I should stay at home over the weekend. I sat there in complete silence, feeling very intimidated, and prayed he would go away, but he stayed for what seemed like a very long time waiting for my response. But then suddenly he left.

I took my sailing kit to work with me the next morning, calm in the knowledge that it would only be a matter of hours before I could put some distance between us.

On the Friday morning before the trip I finally decided to phone our company solicitor and told him I wanted to divorce my husband as quickly as possible. I also instructed him to change my will and said I would collect a copy of it within the hour.

After spending some time with the solicitor I drove to Philip's house. Without telling Philip about the recent events, I asked him to keep an important document safe for me. It was my altered will.

Philip was wonderful, and although some weeks later he told me he was only too aware that I was in great distress at the time, he did not ask me a single question. We loaded his sailing gear into my car and set off to collect Paul. With the two men happily chatting to each other about the forthcoming trip, I slipped into deep thought about my own pressing problems. I was trying hard to sort my mind out when Paul asked me if I was OK.

'I'm just fine.'

'Are you sure? You seem to be very preoccupied.'

Poor man! Without thinking what I was saying, I told him I had no wish to discuss my thoughts with him or anybody else and asked him to kindly leave me in peace.

Going sailing that weekend proved excellent therapy for me. We had arrived in Plymouth by early evening and set about preparing *Kittiwake* to sail down Plymouth Sound.

Philip decided that I should take the first watch, and I soon found myself at the helm trying to avoid the many vessels that were moving about the anchorage. I was not used to sailing in such confined waters and wondered why Philip was entrusting *Kittiwake* to my inexperienced hands. The Tor Point ferry was slowly making its way across the harbour, directly in our path. Nervously I asked how I could avoid hitting it.

'Just continue on your present course and you'll miss it by miles,' Paul assured me.

The two men happily continued their conversation, and as the ferry and *Kittiwake* converged I held my course as bidden. To my amazement, *Kittiwake* passed behind the ferry with room to spare.

During that passage I was to learn a great deal about Paul. He was a natural sailor and an excellent tutor. If I failed to understand any instruction, he would explain it in a simplified form until I grasped it. I asked him if he would be able to come sailing with me on *MacNab*, as I felt sure I could learn a lot from him. He happily agreed, and I felt a strong bond forming between us.

As we approached Land's End the weather deteriorated and conditions became extremely rough. I asked Paul and Philip if this was normal for Land's End, as the first time I had sailed round it on the trip to Roscoff the sea had been flat calm. They both laughed.

'If we'd known it was going to be like this,' one of them said, 'we'd have put into safe harbour until conditions improved.'

During my watch that night, lightning began to shoot across the sky. I had seen no other vessels for two hours, and was afraid that, as *Kittiwake*'s mast was the highest object for miles around, we were in danger of being struck! I waited and worried until ten minutes before my watch was due to end, and then went below and woke Paul.

'You still have ten minutes to go, Paul, but I'm very worried about the weather conditions.'

'OK I'll be there in a moment,' he murmured sleepily.

When he arrived in the cockpit he stared at the lightning. 'Isn't it pretty?' he said innocently.

'Pretty! My God, I've been terrified we'd be struck.'

He pointed to the top of the mast. 'That's a lightning conductor – we've got nothing to worry about.'

I felt really foolish, but as I was still too nervous to go below and sleep I sat in the corner of the cockpit trying to relax. After a while Paul invited me to look over the stern: there in the wake of the yacht were hundreds of bright white lights.

'What is it?' I asked in amazement.

'Phosphorescence. You don't see it very often in these waters, but the Caribbean is alive with it.'

I thanked him for showing me this phenomenon and went below to dream about the Caribbean.

The next afternoon we arrived in Bideford and, after picking up Philip's mooring, we all sat chatting about my plans to build a yacht. I told Paul I was convinced that I wanted to go ahead. There and then, on Philip's boat, I wrote to Bruce Roberts, the yacht designer, enclosing a cheque and requesting a set of plans for a Spray 33. The die was cast!

I never returned to the family home. While I waited to move into a cottage that I had rented, I stayed with friends and started divorce proceedings. I resolved to concentrate solely on my future.

A few weeks after I had moved into my cottage I arrived home from work to find a large package in the front porch. The plans had arrived; I telephoned Paul and he arrived within minutes. I laid a bed sheet on the ground outside, and slowly and carefully we unpacked the parcel. Paul then checked the plans, while I asked a multitude of questions. With each answer my excitement rose. The sheets of plywood that Paul had ordered were waiting in the garage, and the very next morning he arrived with rolls of paper and began lofting the plans out – creating a full-size drawing of the yacht on the plywood from the plans. The construction of *Lucia* had begun!

Over the next few weeks life became more hectic than ever. The steel had by now been delivered to the ship-yard in Appledore, and Paul started welding the frames together. I would call to check on progress as often as I could, sometimes three times a day. I took photos of every single stage, and whenever possible donned a pair of overalls and did whatever I could to assist Paul.

As time progressed and my divorce went from messy to nightmarish, the building of *Lucia* became my lifeline. I was trying very hard to find a buyer for my shares in the business, but my husband seemed to be trying to block my every move so as to leave me short of funds. Yet somehow I knew that I would not be beaten, that I would achieve my dream.

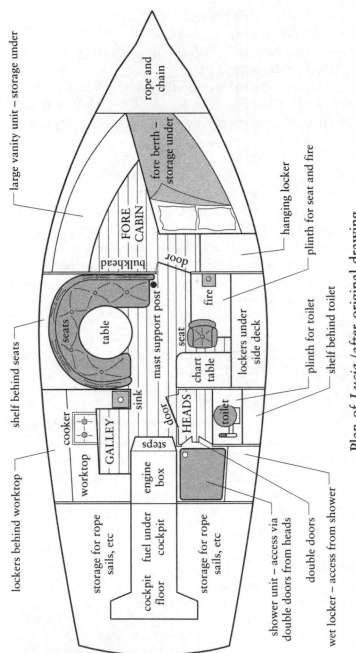

Plan of *Lucia* (after original drawing by Richard Fay of Fay Marine)

large vanity unit – storage under

rope and chain

fore berth – storage under

FORE CABIN

hanging locker

plinth for seat and fire

bulkhead

door

fire

shelf behind seats

seats

table

mast support post

seat

chart table

plinth for toilet

shelf behind toilet

lockers under side deck

sink

HEADS

door

toilet

cooker

GALLEY

steps

worktop

engine box

lockers behind worktop

storage for rope sails, etc

fuel under cockpit

cockpit floor

storage for rope sails, etc

shower unit – access via double doors from heads

double doors

wet locker – access from shower

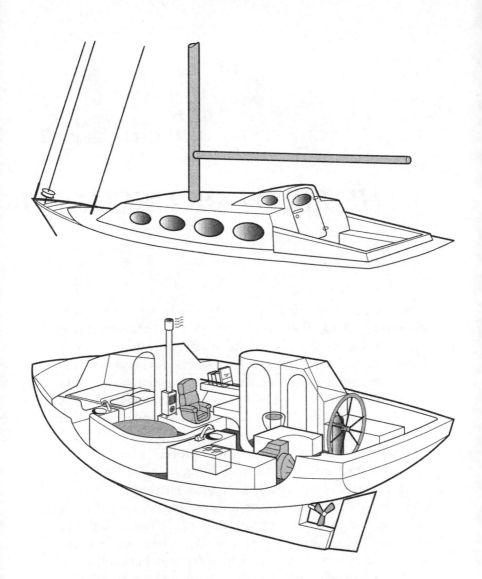

Cross-section of *Lucia* (after original drawing
by Richard Fay of Fay Marine)

CHAPTER THREE

THE BIRTH OF LUCIA

With the financial side of my divorce a long way from agreement, Paul introduced me to the concept of the boat jumble as a way of keeping expenditure down. These fascinating events are markets for second-hand and new equipment for boats and yachts of every description. At six o'clock one Sunday morning, he called to collect me. When I opened the door he looked at me long and hard.

'Don't you have anything else to wear?'

I was shocked. I thought I looked just fine in my black cashmere coat and little flat-heeled shoes.

'Don't you have any jeans and wellington boots?'

I felt aggrieved and brusquely told him I did not possess a pair of jeans and didn't think wellingtons would go with my coat. We then drove a hundred miles to an extremely wet, boggy field in South Wales. Although I was, of course, far from suitably dressed, I had a wonderful time. The first thing I purchased, not surprisingly, was a pair of sailing boots.

Every stall we visited was a source of education. Paul would pick up an article, explain what it was and how it worked, then tell me how many I needed. Having bought bits and pieces for himself at a number of places, he collected up a few items for me from one stall and handed them to me so that I could pay for them. I asked the stallholder the price of each and then began to bargain. Paul, finding this a little embarrassing, started to edge away, but when I managed to buy the lot for a quarter of the asking price he looked at me in amazement.

Once out of earshot he exclaimed, 'You obviously have no idea what things are worth – I don't know how you got them so cheap! From now on I'll tell you what to buy and you do the dealing .... By the way, would you mind buying a few things for me as well?'

We devised a code. Paul would examine the gear, and if he took his car keys out of his pocket it meant that particular item was wanted by one of us and I would go into action. As a result *Lucia* became more affordable, and Paul was able to start buying parts for the proposed building of his own new yacht sooner than he had expected.

During *Lucia*'s construction we attended well over forty of these boat jumbles. We jokingly called ourselves 'jumble junkies' and soon built up a rapport with the stallholders. Some of them used to groan good-naturedly when we approached, while others were very encouraging and seemed genuinely interested in the building of *Lucia*. My knowledge of yacht parts grew in leaps and bounds.

Five months after I moved out of the family home my divorce eventually came through, but my ex-husband found it hard to accept that now he had less right than ever to interfere with my life.

Unfortunately, I was still working full time in our jointly-owned business and he had plenty of opportunity to make my life as difficult as he could. The office became unbearable, and I longed for the day when I would find a buyer for my shares and get out. At one point I almost gave my ex-husband my shares as I felt I could not take any more. My working life had become so traumatic that I just wanted out of the situation. It was only the support of my family and friends, especially Russel, Paul and Philip, that stopped me going insane.

I did eventually obtain a court ruling ordering my ex-husband to comply with certain conditions, one of which was not to contact me during the hours of 6p.m. to 9a.m. But even on the day of the court's decision, he broke this part of the ruling. I knew then that with or without the court order I would never be free of this man, so I went full speed ahead to distance myself from the situation in both mind and body.

Paul would come sailing with me as often as he could. As *MacNab* was moored in a tidal estuary we could only sail at certain times. When I knew the tide would be right, no matter how inclement the weather, I would telephone Paul and plead with him to meet me and give me another sailing lesson. Sometimes he would groan and say, 'But it's raining' or '. . . blowing a gale'. I would always reply that it was only raining a little, or 'Well, it's not down here.' Looking back, I realise there must have been times when it was the last thing Paul wanted to do.

One lesson I will never forget. It was a bad day for me emotionally, and when Paul arrived that evening, as arranged, I really did not want to go sailing.

'Come on, it will do you good. You know sailing always makes you feel better,' he encouraged. I had to agree with him, and within the hour we were sailing up the river towards Bideford quay.

Paul said it was about time I learnt to sail up to a quay rather than use the engine, and asked me to come alongside at a certain point. I sailed *MacNab* towards the quay, waiting until the very last moment to turn so that I would be as close as possible. Paul felt sure I was going to hit the quay and yelled at me to turn immediately. I did so, and this left us a few feet off the quay.

'See, I was right!' I said cheekily.

We tacked back across the river and Paul asked me to repeat the manoeuvre. This time he walked towards the bow and told me that I was completely in charge. He was not going to give me any instructions and if I hit the quay it was down to me. I held my course, turning at the last moment, and came alongside the quay with just inches to spare. Paul stepped ashore and pushed *MacNab* away from the quay as he went.

'Now do it all again and come back and pick me up,' he said, laughing.

I was shocked. 'How could you do this to me?' I demanded in horror. It was too late, of course. I was on my own!

I was concentrating so hard on the wind direction and the set of the sails that I failed to notice the rowers practising racing starts until their boat was very close to my bow. The skipper of their support launch started shouting rude words at me. I replied that I had right of way as I was under sail. But the skipper kept shouting at me, and the rowers made no attempt to slow down or change course. To avoid hitting them I had to tack and go back across the river once more before attempting the exercise again. When I eventually came alongside and picked Paul up, he gave me a big hug and said he was delighted with me. He also confirmed that I was correct and did indeed have right of way. It was only then that my legs turned to jelly.

Some weeks previously Paul had asked me how I reacted in an emergency. Did I panic, or did I do something positive? I really could not give him an answer. But after the incident with the rowers Paul said he would have no worries about me crossing the Atlantic, as I had acted in a very positive way during that emergency. By the time we arrived back at the mooring, my earlier depression had lifted completely and elation had taken its place.

My financial situation was becoming desperate. If I was going to continue to build *Lucia* I had to find some way of raising money. The only asset over which I had control at that time was *MacNab*. In one way I was very lucky – she sold very quickly. But then I had no vessel in which to have sailing lessons. I missed *MacNab* dreadfully after I had tearfully delivered her to her new owner.

Not long after the sale Robin Sealey, the local chandler, heard from Paul that I was having withdrawal symptoms because I no longer had a vessel to sail. He very kindly lent me his Silhouette class of yacht called *Rag Doll* – a small wooden sailing craft with a tiny cabin. It had a Seagull outboard engine that I could never start, so I was forced to improve my sailing skills.

Rag Doll was on a mooring in a part of the river known as Snuffy Corner, where the wind would either die completely or turn completely around which is known as 'boxing the compass'. One day Paul was standing on the shore, watching my painfully slow progress as I tried in vain to return *Rag Doll* to her mooring. I looked his way just as he cupped his hands around his mouth. Wonderful, I thought, here come words of wisdom. Then, to my great amusement, he yelled at the top of his voice, 'Sail the bloody thing!' Far be it from me to disobey my tutor's instructions. I turned *Rag Doll* until the wind caught in her sails and successfully brought her to the mooring. I picked it up and yelled back at Paul.

'Like that, you mean!'

The money I received from the sale of *MacNab* went to complete *Lucia*'s hull and deck, to buy materials to

start fitting her out and to pay wages. Paul had recommended Peter Robbins to fit out *Lucia*'s interior; he had
known Peter for many years and had a great respect for
his skills and ability. Unfortunately, it was not long
before the coffers were reduced to their previous level.
Although Peter had progressed well with the interior
joinery, I had no choice but to lay him off until my
situation improved.

Then I had a remarkable piece of good luck. The
manager of a paint company who was working on some
of the commercial vessels in the shipyard had taken a
great interest in *Lucia* and offered to supply the materials
and paint her free of charge. Once *Lucia* was painted,
Paul advised me to save money by moving her from the
shipyard to the garden of my rented cottage.

'It'll be a tight fit, but I'll still be able to work on her,
as long as I have a power supply,' he said.

I approached my landlord with trepidation, feeling sure
he would turn down my request. To my delight he agreed
whole-heartedly. Then I wondered how my neighbours
would react. But I need not have worried – once *Lucia* was
installed they all took great interest in her progress.

A few weeks later Paul came into my kitchen while I
was on the telephone and gestured that he wanted to
make a cup of coffee. After looking in the fridge he
began to open and close the kitchen cupboards. I
wondered why. When I had finished my call, he said he
wanted to talk to me.

'Money's very short, isn't it?' Your cupboards and
fridge are almost bare.'

My heart sank. I wondered if he was going to stop
working on *Lucia* for fear I would be unable to pay
him. 'It's OK. I just haven't had time to go shopping,' I
lied.

'Really? Is that why you're looking so thin? Let's sit
down and discuss this, shall we?'

We spent the next few hours calculating the cost of materials and wages to bring *Lucia* to a stage at which she could be launched and lived aboard. When we compared the total to my savings and income there was quite a shortfall. I thought work on *Lucia* would have to come to a complete standstill until I received my divorce settlement or sold my business shares.

'That's not a good idea,' Paul responded. 'If we call a halt now, I know it will be much harder to restart. It will be better if we can keep the project ticking over.'

He started doing some more calculations, then amazed me by saying, 'I need very little to live on. If you could pay me £50 a week and owe me the rest of my wages until your situation improves, I can continue to work on *Lucia*. With this arrangement it will mean that you can eat as well!' I found Paul's kindness and understanding beyond belief, and accepted his offer with extreme gratitude.

One evening a few weeks later, Paul called to say he was on his way to see me with Peter, as there was something urgent they needed to discuss. Peter explained that he and his partner Anita had applied to emigrate to Australia.

'The one thing I really want to complete before I leave is the work on *Lucia*,' he said.

I explained that I would love him to do so, but there was no way I could pay him.

'Paul's told me of the arrangement you've come to over his wages, and I can go one better. I don't need you to pay me anything. I'll give you an invoice at the end of each week, and you can pay me when you've sold your shares,' he offered.

'But that could be months. You may even be in Australia by then,' I replied.

'That doesn't matter. I'll treat what you owe me as savings.'

I looked at Paul in astonishment and said, 'I don't know what to say.'

'Why don't you try "thank you",' he advised.

I did so, and the three of us fell into fits of laughter.

This arrangement had only one flaw. I desperately needed money for materials and, much to my family and friend's astonishment, I put up for auction all but a few necessary items of furniture and personal effects. From that moment on, progress was very swift. Watching *Lucia* reach the final stages of her construction was wonderful. Each evening when I had finished work I would climb aboard to check on her progress: my dream was now fast becoming a reality.

I had started yet another navigation class, this time Ocean Master. The course included astro navigation, which at first was way above my head. I had to learn how to use a sextant to obtain the angle of the sun, stars or planets in relation to the horizon, and then use this measurement along with tables of logarithms to calculate the vessel's position at sea. Night after night I studied and struggled with the subject. Slowly it became clearer and I began to understand what I was doing. My confidence grew and I managed to pass the exam. On reflection, I often wondered where I got the energy and determination to complete so many things in such a small space of time.

Christmas was fast approaching and, although *Lucia* was still firmly on dry land, I resolved if possible to celebrate by having Christmas dinner aboard. Peter was unhappy about this prospect and asked my son to try and dissuade me. When I asked Peter why he was objecting he confessed that he was worried I would damage his work! I promised him I would be very careful and gently reminded him that *Lucia* was soon going to be my home, that I was going sail her alone and that she would have to endure a great deal more than a Christmas dinner.

Russel and I had a wonderful Christmas day. We laughed a great deal about the fact that, although there was plenty of water around, it was falling from the sky instead of flowing beneath us. While he slept off his enormous meal, I began to daydream about all the Christmas days of the future. I imagined gently rocking in a beautiful anchorage while enjoying warm sunshine, blue skies and crystal-clear sea. I was longing for the day when I could set sail.

At the beginning of February *Lucia* was almost ready for launch, and the tide would be right in two weeks' time. I arranged for the crane and transportation to arrive early on the morning of the 20th, which turned out to be one of the coldest, windiest, wettest days imaginable. However, the dreadful weather did not deter family, friends and neighbours from showing up to witness this momentous occasion. There was a great air of excitement as we watched *Lucia* being plucked from the garden and skilfully loaded on to the flatbed lorry. Thankfully, she suffered no ill effects from the high winds and driving rain.

In a convoy of assorted vehicles we followed Lucia on her short journey to Bideford, where she was lifted from the lorry and suspended over the quay. Then Paul and I climbed aboard and handed lines to willing hands on the shore. As she hung there in the slings of the crane, Philip made a marvellous speech and at the second attempt broke a bottle of champagne over her bows. To great cheers from the onlookers, *Lucia* was gently lowered into the river Torridge. The slings were removed and she was, at last, in her natural element. Paul started the engine and asked me to test the gears, first forward and then reverse. All was well and I stood to one side, expecting him to take the helm.

'No,' he insisted. 'It's your boat's first trip, so you must take the helm.'

This took me completely by surprise. The mooring lines were thrown on board and, with a dry mouth and a pumping heart, I steered *Lucia* slowly towards the centre of the river. I turned her in a complete circle, first to check the steering and secondly to be sure I could helm by wheel, as this was a first for me. Up until that moment I had only ever helmed by tiller. *Lucia* responded very well and, still nervous but delighted with her performance, I took her up the river to her mooring.

Once she was secured we went below to try and thaw out. My fingers were frozen and it took me ages to light the gas cooker in order to bring a little warmth in to the cabin. Once Paul was happy that she was safely settled, we launched the dinghy and went ashore. As I looked back at *Lucia* floating happily on her mooring, I felt she had come alive. I promised her a life she could be proud of.

CHAPTER FOUR

MAIDEN VOYAGE

The next day we moved *Lucia* into the tidal dock that was to become her home for a few months. Access from the land was across a muddy field to the wall enclosing the berth, then a descent via a twelve-foot builder's ladder on to her deck. Getting aboard when the tide was in was not too difficult, but at low tide the trek up and down the ladder took a bit of getting used to.

I transferred all my possessions on board, swiftly filling every locker and available space. Then I moved myself aboard and tried to adjust my lifestyle to my new surroundings. At first I was in a complete and utter muddle; there were far too many items crammed into the lockers and finding anything was a marathon task. Realising that this could not continue, I removed all the 'one day this will come in handy' items and gave them to my family and friends.

Under Paul's instructions, whenever weather and tide would permit during the winter I took *Lucia* up and down the river to practise manoeuvring her under power. Paul would mark out an imaginary marina against the walls of Bideford bridge, and I would have to bring *Lucia* alongside in as many different ways as he could think of. This did not come easily to me, and at the end of each lesson I was exhausted. I often wondered how on earth I would manage in a real marina.

Winter was not the best time to begin life afloat, but once I got organised I loved it. My father and Paul had built a wonderful solid fuel fire for me, which kept *Lucia* very warm and cosy. However, hauling bags of coal across the field and down the ladder was not my favourite task. But there was a silver lining – my body was getting a good workout! As I was still working full time, one of the most difficult things was to appear at the office looking respectable. My car became a mobile wardrobe, carrying smart shoes and a variety of clothes that I could easily change into.

As winter turned into spring, I found a buyer for my shares at last. These things take time and patience, but slowly the transaction progressed. The effect was amazing. At last I felt free to pursue my aims, knowing I would soon be able to pay off my debts and finish *Lucia*, transforming her from a houseboat into a sailing yacht.

Paul and I had been talking for some time to Eurospars, the people who were going to supply *Lucia*'s rig, and now I was in a position to confirm my order. Early in June we took *Lucia* up the river to Appledore shipyard to have her mast stepped.

Once more I asked Brian, the owner of Kas Cranes, to use his excellent skills to lift *Lucia*'s forty-five-foot mast over her deck. Peter from Eurospars, along with two assistants and Paul secured it in place and *Lucia* was totally transformed. This was another red-letter day that was full of magic. With her rig in place she looked, as she should, a beautiful ocean sailing yacht. I went to sleep that night full of hope and joy.

When Paul arrived the following morning to fit the

outer furling system he casually asked me if I would winch him up the mast. I was horrified – Paul is a big man, and there would be no way I could hold him on a rope if something went wrong.

'I think it would be better if I went,' I said nervously.

'Are you sure? It's a long way up and you've never done it before.'

'I'm sure I'll hate it, but I'd much prefer the climb than to be responsible for your life!'

Paul explained that I had to take the tape measure to a certain spot on the mast and gently drop it to the deck, so that he could measure the length of the fore stay. I put on my harness and Paul tied the main halyard to the ring at the front.

'Make sure it's a good knot – I don't want it coming undone,' I instructed. He laughed and assured me I would be fine.

I needed help to climb on to the boom, as the bottom mast step was still to be fitted. Just standing on the boom felt extremely dangerous. But as I looked up the forty-five feet to the top of my mast my stomach turned several somersaults. Nevertheless I knew I had to do it. I took a few deep breaths and started my ascent. Reaching up to the step above my head, I held on tightly as I carefully fitted my foot into the first step. I continued in this vein until I reached the spot from where I had to start the measurement. A few moments after I had lowered the tape, Paul yelled up from the deck.

'OK, I've got what I need. You can come down now.'

As I reached the boom and felt Paul's strong arms lift me off, my legs started to wobble. He told me to go and make some tea while he marked off the measurement along the furling system.

'Then we'll be ready to hoist it up the mast and fit it in place,' he said with a big smile on his face.

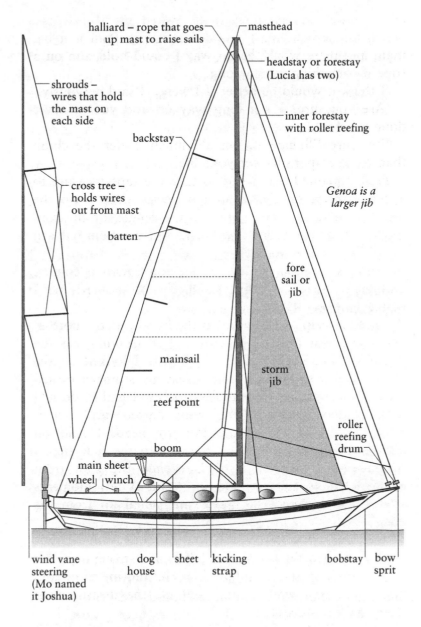

halliard – rope that goes up mast to raise sails

masthead

headstay or forestay (Lucia has two)

shrouds – wires that hold the mast on each side

inner forestay with roller reefing

backstay

Genoa is a larger jib

cross tree – holds wires out from mast

batten

fore sail or jib

mainsail

storm jib

reef point

roller reefing drum

boom

main sheet

wheel   winch

wind vane steering (Mo named it Joshua)

dog house

sheet

kicking strap

bobstay

bow sprit

Diagram of *Lucia* showing her sails (after original drawing by Richard Fay of Fay Marine)

An hour later Paul asked me how I felt about going up again, as this time I would have to use both hands to operate the tools and secure the fitting. I assured him I felt the same as last time – I would much rather do the job, than be responsible for him. The second time around I was even more concerned for my safety; I felt it was a bit like giving birth – after you've done it once you know what to expect!

Paul had tied all the tools I needed to use on to my harness, and I put the fittings and a split pin in my pocket. When I reached the top of the mast, I wrapped my legs and arms very tightly around it and tried not to look down. By now I had made up my mind not to waste any effort on worrying what would happen if I fell, but to concentrate on getting the job done right as quickly as possible. When I called to Paul to tell him I had completed the task he surprised me.

'Just stay there for a few more seconds, Mo,' he shouted back. 'I want to take a picture of you up there.'

'That's not a good idea at all, Paul! I'm coming down right now – to hell with your photo,' I yelled. I heard laughter, and looked down to see a group of the shipyard workers enjoying the spectacle immensely.

Back on deck once again I started to shake and felt extremely tired. Paul made the tea this time. By now I was certain I would never enjoy climbing the mast, but at least I knew I was capable of doing so when the need arose. The next day my arms and legs were a mass of bruises where I had been tightly gripping the mast.

Not long after the mast was stepped, the sails arrived and we bent them on. Now *Lucia* was ready for her first test sail. As soon as conditions would permit, with Paul, his son Richard and Philip on board we ventured out into the river. As *Lucia* glided through the water I felt so happy I thought I would burst. She sailed like a dream! That evening we had a wonderful celebration party and afterwards I had great difficulty falling asleep, as my mind was so full of plans for the future.

Falmouth, some thirty hours from her mooring in Bideford, was chosen as the destination for *Lucia*'s shakedown voyage. We would sail along the Bristol Channel to Land's End, rounding the furthest point of land into the English Channel, then past Mousehole, Newlyn, Penzance and the Lizard, and finally on to Falmouth. Night after night I dreamt about this voyage, sometimes waking full of confidence, at other times full of trepidation.

My days were unbelievably hectic as I tied up the loose ends of my divorce and the sale of my shares. I felt like a permanent fixture in the solicitor's office. Whenever I had a spare moment I was stocking up lockers with food and whatever else I considered necessary for the forthcoming trip. The nights were just as difficult: my mind was full to bursting and sleeping was becoming a problem. The appointed day of departure was rushing towards me and I felt sure I would not be ready.

Paul and Philip, along with Charlie, the young man who had fitted *Lucia*'s electronic equipment, were to join me for the trip. They arrived on the morning of departure and found me still with a lot to do. The previous night, on Paul's advice, I had taken a sleeping pill. Although I had slept for a good eight hours, I had woken up feeling extremely heavy and groggy. My mind was trying to function through a thick fog. It was, to say the least, a bit of a scramble to leave the mooring before the tide went out and left us high and dry. Paul was not happy about this: leaving when the tide had ebbed too far meant that we would be fighting against the tide all the way, instead of using it to our advantage.

Young Charlie described the trip as a baptism of fire, and it was not that much of an exaggeration. One after the other we fell foul to seasickness. I got very tired as I tried to take in all that Paul was trying to teach me. There were very few quiet moments, apart from two hours during the late afternoon when I kept watch while the three men went to sleep.

The next day, as we were fighting the tide to round Land's End, Paul and Philip began to get very short-tempered with each other. I did not enjoy this unpleasant atmosphere at all, and did my best to keep the peace by trying to obey the instructions given to me by both of them. This proved to be a big mistake. While Paul and Charlie were attending to some minor problem at the mast, Paul told me to put the electronic autopilot on. Philip, who was in the cockpit with me, suddenly instructed me to switch off the autopilot and take the helm myself as *Lucia* was in danger of performing a Chinese jibe – whatever that was! Within seconds, Paul asked me what had happened to the autopilot.

'Nothing,' I replied. 'Philip told me to turn it off and take the helm myself.' The ensuing shouting match between the two of them came as a great shock to me. Philip went into a deep sulk and Paul's ill temper reached new heights. With these two not talking to each other, an uneasy stalemate settled over *Lucia* like a damp blanket.

We had just passed the Manacles buoy when I slipped in the cockpit and put my knee out (an old skiing injury). Charlie went below to find my knee harness and a packet of frozen peas to reduce the swelling. Paul demanded to know who was skipper of the boat, complaining: 'This trip is going from bad to worse – there has to be just one person in charge.' Philip took this personally and went below, extremely upset. I appointed Paul skipper and then struggled down the companion-way on my bottom to comfort Philip. By now I was extremely concerned that they would never speak to each other again. When I managed to return to the cockpit, I told Paul that at the first opportunity he should make his peace with Philip. Within minutes he disappeared below and after a short time they both emerged. They were still not exactly the best of friends, but at least the atmosphere was a little lighter.

Paul issued instructions to prepare *Lucia* for harbour, and an hour later we came alongside the holding pontoon at the Falmouth Yacht Marina. After being told where we could berth *Lucia* Paul turned to me and asked if I would like him to take her in.

'Oh, yes please.'

'OK, but you must closely watch everything I do. Next time you'll be doing this on your own.'

I watched him with every fibre of my body taut, and to my amazement he promptly hit another boat.

'Well, not quite like that,' he said as a big smile spread across his face. Thankfully, neither yacht had sustained any damage.

Once we were safely secured, we went below to have a drink and a meal and conduct a post-mortem on *Lucia*'s maiden voyage. The conclusion was reached that she had performed very well, despite difficult conditions and a rebellious crew! I have to admit that after the three men had returned to Bideford, leaving me in Falmouth, I breathed a sigh of relief. I had been rushing around for weeks and I desperately needed to rest in order to recharge my batteries. I spent the next few days getting to know my new surroundings and thinking about *Lucia*'s next voyage.

Soon enough I was ready to crack on with the many jobs awaiting my attention, the most urgent of which was to get my compass adjusted. I arranged for Graham, a local compass adjuster, to call, and on the appointed day I was up very early. This was mostly due to my nerves, since this would be the first time I had manoeuvred *Lucia* in and out of a marina. I prayed that Paul's tuition would not fail me. By the time the unsuspecting Graham arrived I had started the engine and prepared *Lucia* for departure.

Maybe it was beginner's luck, but I was greatly relieved when we slipped out of the berth as if I had done it a hundred times before. Once out in the bay I manoeuvred *Lucia* as required, while the adjuster took bearings off various landmarks and compared them to *Lucia*'s compass. After repeated efforts Graham gave up and said he would take the compass back to his workshop to see what the problem was. (It later transpired that my second-hand compass had irreparable faults, and I had to purchase a new one.) As we returned to the marina I wondered how I would fare bringing *Lucia* back into her berth. It was not a perfect entry, but I did manage to bring her safely in. I got a very old-fashioned look from Graham when I said I needed a strong drink and I didn't mean tea! Having successfully piloted *Lucia* in and out of the marina, I could not wait to call Paul and tell him his hours of patience had not been wasted.

We were planning to take *Lucia* to the Channel Islands as soon as Paul could arrange some free time. He promised to be just an observer and not to give me any advice or instruction unless he thought we were in danger. I had missed Paul greatly while I was in Falmouth, and was longing to see him again. We had become close friends over the two years that we had known each other, and very slowly our friendship had blossomed into one of lovers – though at first we were both reluctant to accept this situation and tried hard to avoid the inevitable. Having a man in my life was the last thing I needed, but Paul was so unlike any man I had ever known. He had a great respect for women and, although he knew there were huge differences between the male and female psyche, he accepted these differences. He showed no desire to clip my wings and took great pleasure in the progress I was making as I launched myself into my new way of life. His support and encouragement intensified my love for him.

In the time leading up to *Lucia*'s next departure I continued to enjoy life in Falmouth. It was an inspiring place to be in. There were two types of sailors in the marina, those who dreamt about the cruising life and those who were actually participating in it. Every day yachts arrived on their way to or from different parts of the world. Some of the dreamers had been in Falmouth for years but for one reason or another would never make the giant leap. I met people from both groups, but of course it was the cruising folk who drew me like a magnet. I would soak up stories of their sailing exploits and learn all I could about the places they had visited. I never once doubted that I would soon join their ranks.

Just before *Lucia* set off again Russel came for a short visit and to help me with some last-minute jobs. When Paul arrived on the Friday evening, Russel and I had almost completed preparations for the trip. That evening we had a super farewell meal in the marina restaurant before Russel reluctantly returned to North Devon. I knew he would have loved to accompany us, but because I was treating this as a single-handed training trip I felt it was essential to have only Paul on board.

Later that evening I worked on my passage plan and navigation; Paul confirmed that it was correct. Needless to say, I had trouble getting to sleep that night as my mind was alive with excitement and anticipation. The next morning, to my relief, the weather forecast was favourable, so I posted the customs form as required by law when leaving a British port for a foreign harbour, and said farewell to the many friends I had made during my stay in the marina. Then Paul and I set sail for the Channel Islands.

It was a beautiful day and, once clear of St Anthony's Head, with Paul watching my every move I put *Lucia* on course. Then I set the self-steering and trimmed the sails until I felt satisfied that she was sailing along beautifully. I sat in the cockpit, feeling apprehensive still but very happy. I plotted my course every hour or so on the chart. Doing all the work myself, I was amazed how quickly the time passed.

As day turned to evening, the wind freshened and I wondered how soon I should put in a reef. Paul had gone below to have a sleep, and I felt very unsure of what to do. By 2300 hours I had decided to reduce the size of the main sail by putting in a reef and attempted to do so. Within minutes Paul appeared and asked me what I was doing.

'Putting a reef in.'

He asked the question again, and I gave the same response while struggling with the task.

Eventually Paul exclaimed, 'What *are* you doing, woman?'

'Obviously making a complete hash of trying to put a reef in.'

'You're right. Why haven't you put the deck lights on?'

'I didn't want to disturb you.'

'I don't believe it! I'm not here, remember – you're meant to be on your own. Now act as if you are.'

I rushed below and put the deck lights on. What a difference it made with some light on the subject. Now I could see that the sail was still full of wind – I had forgotten to let the main sheet go. I corrected this immediately, put the reef in and very soon *Lucia* was under control once more. Paul returned below, reminding me as he went that he was not there and the only thing I was to give consideration to was *Lucia*.

By dawn I was feeling very tired, not having dared to close my eyes because the English Channel is such a busy stretch of water. Paul appeared once more and asked me where and when I expected to see land. I answered this to the best of my ability and he disappeared back below. At the appointed time, Paul reappeared and scanned the horizon with the binoculars.

'Land, just where and when you said it would be,' he announced.

I grabbed the binoculars from him, hardly daring to believe my eyes. 'Guernsey,' I exclaimed.

'Well, we don't know that yet. It could be anywhere. At the moment all we know is that it's land.'

I plotted the position on the chart and showed it to Paul, assuring him that the land we could see just had to be Guernsey. Paul was highly amused at how seriously I had taken his comments. I was aglow with the knowledge that I had managed to navigate *Lucia* accurately, and this magical feeling banished all traces of tiredness. Paul and I sat in the cockpit drinking tea and chatting away quite happily, and then his face took on a serious expression.

'Mo, I've decided I won't return to Falmouth with you.'

I shot him a look of complete surprise. 'Why on earth not?'

'Philip and I have taught you all we can. You've proved to me that somewhere in your mind you've stored this knowledge. Although you lack experience, it's time you set sail without me.'

I remonstrated with him for imparting this news at that particular moment, spoiling my euphoric mood. But although I needed a great deal of reassurance he was right, and this did indeed prove to be the correct course of action.

Some hours later we dropped anchor in the beautiful

bay of Petit Port, Guernsey. It was so idyllic that we decided to stay overnight and go into St Peter Port the next day. We spent a wonderful evening, eating supper and sipping drinks in the cockpit, while we watched the setting sun. Life to me at that moment was close to perfect.

The next morning, as we approached St Peter Port, I called Port Control on the VHF radio. I was instructed to make for a certain buoy and wait for the harbour patrol boat, which would direct me to a berth in the marina. I thought at first that they were doing this specially for me. It was only as I made my way towards the appointed buoy that I realised *Lucia* was just one of many yachts, but it does no harm to have occasional delusions of grandeur.

Before long there was a stream of yachts queuing up in orderly fashion in front and behind *Lucia*. Although I felt Paul would rather manoeuvre *Lucia* himself into what was obviously a very crowded marina, I pleaded with him to let me do this without instruction.

'OK,' he agreed. 'On one condition – you tell me what you're planning to do every step of the way.'

As I slowly followed the yacht in front, a French vessel left the holding pontoon to my right with every intention of cutting in front of *Lucia*. I fixed the man on the helm with a look of pure horror: was he really going to risk a collision? Whatever he deduced from my expression I shall never know, but after a few moments he beat a hasty retreat. I looked at Paul as I breathed a sigh of relief.

'You'll come across a lot of idiots like that,' he assured me. 'Don't let them faze you.'

I swallowed hard and continued to keep my place in the queue. Because *Lucia* had a shallow draft we could manoeuvre well into the inner harbour. My mouth grew drier as the tension built. We were eventually directed to a pontoon in front of the main road running through St Peter Port. I came alongside it without a hitch and Paul stepped ashore to secure the lines. Within a few minutes the customs officers came aboard, and once the relevant documents were completed Paul and I were left alone for a quick debriefing.

'Didn't I do well?' I said proudly.

'With the customs men?'

'No, you idiot – bringing *Lucia* into the berth.'

'You did OK.'

'OK? *OK?* It was absolutely marvellous,' I exclaimed. We fell upon each other in fits of laughter. I felt on top of the world and was bursting with exhilaration.

Paul and I spent a few blissful days together exploring Guernsey and meeting some of the people on other yachts. Then with lightning speed the day he was due to fly back to England arrived and we said a tearful farewell. I spent the next few months in the Channel Islands and, although I enjoyed my life afloat immensely, I did miss Paul dreadfully.

Just before I returned to Falmouth my two sons joined me for a holiday and we had a great time together sailing and partying. Colin had to fly back to England before Russel, and while Russel and I were discussing my passage across the English Channel he asked if he could come with me. My first response was to refuse, explaining that it was one thing to risk my life but quite another to risk his. But after a couple of hours, listening to Russel's reasons why he wanted to accompany me, I gave in, albeit reluctantly.

I planned my return voyage with great care, checking my navigation over and over again. I phoned Paul to ask his opinion of the weather forecast. He advised me to leave sooner rather than later, which matched my own feelings. I decided that we would leave the following day. Russel went out on the town that evening with

John, an Australian yachtie he had befriended, and judging from the state of him the next morning he had a wonderful time. John and his partner Helen were planning to leave for France that morning, and I hoped that John was in better shape than Russel.

I left Russel sleeping for as long as I could while I completed last-minute jobs to get *Lucia* ready to set sail. When I did eventually wake him, all that was left to do was to slip the lines. I thought I was extremely calm and had everything well organised. I started the engine and went forward to tell Russel the order in which I wanted him to slip the lines. I returned to the cockpit and stood behind the helm – but something was missing. With horror I realised that I had forgotten to replace the steering wheel, which I had removed while in harbour to give more room in the cockpit.

'Hold everything, Russel! I yelled as I went forward to retrieve the wheel from the top of the deck.

'You really sure you're up to this, Mum?' Russel said, laughing. I felt such a fool!

After taking a few deep breaths, we left the pontoon very smoothly and made our way over the sill to the holding pontoon in the outer harbour to await our late afternoon departure. John and Helen were moored just in front of *Lucia* and Helen called over to us to join them for breakfast. By the time we went aboard John had retired to his bunk again to sleep off his hangover. Helen felt sure their departure would have to be delayed.

Later that day, by the time that *Lucia* slipped away from Guernsey, my confidence had returned after my earlier blunder and Russel had almost recovered from his binge the previous night. I was concerned that he would become anxious as night fell and we lost sight of land, but luckily my fears were unfounded and he appeared totally relaxed. He ate and slept as if he had not a care in the world, and showed no sign of seasickness. As for me – well, somebody had to feed the fish, didn't they?

Visibility was not that good, and I was disappointed that the wonderful night sky I had often described to Russel was going to be denied to him. While I was keeping a really good look out for other shipping, Russel popped up from down below, looked around for a few minutes and said he was surprised there appeared to be so little out there. It was only during the early hours of the morning, when visibility improved and the lights from other vessels were everywhere, that Russel understood what we were up against.

Russel later suggested I try and get some sleep. As *Lucia* was sailing along really well and I had not needed to adjust anything for the past few hours, I agreed. I lay down in the cockpit, so that all Russ had to do was nudge me if he was concerned about anything. I had just drifted off when what can only be described as an explosion made me leap out of my skin. Russel and I looked at each other in utter shock. Yet there was nothing to explain this incident. We did discuss the possibility that World War III might have started and nobody had informed us. However, the cause of this extraordinary noise remained a mystery. None the less, the effect was to banish my desire to sleep for the rest of the voyage!

During our passage across the English Channel, Russel and I enjoyed the luxury of being able to discuss many things without interruption for hours. We are more than mother and son; we have always been good friends who are unafraid of being very frank with each other. Russ confided in me that he was hopeful his relationship with Rhiannon, a young woman he had been friends with for a short time, would soon blossom. As soon as my mobile phone was in range he called her, and took great pleasure in telling her he was sailing in the middle of the English Channel.

As the voyage progressed I was continually plotting our position on the chart, hopeful that my navigation would prove to be accurate. By late afternoon I was scanning the horizon when I spotted land off our starboard bow. A great sense of achievement welled up inside me. I called Russel to share this magical moment and was surprised that he seemed unaffected by it.

'Aren't you amazed that I managed to find land?'

'Of course not, Mum. I have every confidence in your ability.'

'You have? Foolish boy.' I laughed. I have to admit Russel's trust in me was a terrific boost.

While Russel kept watch, I studied the chart. Night was approaching and, although arriving at Falmouth during the hours of darkness was unavoidable, it was not something I was looking forward to. While living in Falmouth I had navigated in and out of the harbour a few times in daylight, and I remembered there were some unmistakable landmarks. But at night, I knew, things would look completely different. I explained to Russel how I planned to make the approach, and pointed out the page I had marked in the Cruising Association book.

After identifying the Lizard light, we continued on our course towards St Anthony's Head and the river Fal. One hazard just inside the entrance to the river is Black Rock. This is marked by an unlit buoy, and I made sure that our course would keep it well to port. While Russel was down below looking at the chart we safely passed this hazard. Slowly I made my way towards the next mark, a starboard hand buoy. Russel appeared in the cockpit with the book opened at the appropriate page.

'Mum, there's a thing here called Black Rock. We'll have to make sure we miss that.'

'It's OK, darling, I'm pretty sure I know where that is.' Bless him, he looked around just in time to see the starboard hand buoy as we were approaching it.

'*Mum*!!!'

A second later the buoy was lit up by its green light which reflected in Russel's face, highlighting his look of horror. I could not help laughing, but my jovial mood did not last long. Now I had to find the next point of reference, which with the backdrop of lights from the shore proved to be very difficult.

The phone rang. Russel rushed below to answer it, returning with it to the cockpit.

'It's Paul for you, Mum.'

'I can't possibly talk to him now, darling. Tell him I'll call him when we get in.'

Russel disregarded my protest and pushed the phone into my hand. I repeated my comments to Paul.

'Of course you can talk to me. Where are you?'

'St Anthony's Head is astern, and we've just passed the starboard hand buoy.'

'Great. Now I can stop worrying – you're almost there.'

'What are you talking about? I've still got the worst bit to come. I've got to get down this river.'

'You'll be fine. Go carefully and I'll phone you in the morning.' I handed the phone back to Russel, wishing I shared Paul's confidence in me.

The next hour and a half was extremely stressful as we inched our way down the river. At one point I decided to end the torment for the night and pick up a mooring buoy. Russel was up at the bows trying to spot the red can buoys that mark the channel leading to the Falmouth Yacht Marina.

'Shine the torch to the right, Russ, and see if we can spot a mooring buoy.'

Russel turned towards me, inadvertently shining the

torch in my eyes and blinding me. Every time he turned to talk to me he gave me a repeat of this blinding experience until I yelled at him.

'OK, Mum, no need to shout. Look just there – will that one do?' Russel was shining the torch on a very suspect-looking buoy just ahead and to the right of us.

'Do your best to hook it, darling,' I replied.

He was successful, but as soon as we were lying to the buoy I realised we would have to let it go. We were swinging far too close to the nearest boat.

'Sorry, Russ, you'll have to let it go.' He seemed to be a long time setting us free, and immediately we were he rushed below to wash his hands.

'Russ, what on earth are you doing? I need you up forward with the torch. We've just got to find the channel buoys!'

'I'll explain later, Mum,' he said as he made his way to the bow. Thankfully, within a few moments he spotted the first buoy, and with great relief we arrived at the holding pontoon fifteen minutes later. As soon as we were tied up I went below and collapsed in the chair. It was 1.30a.m., and the trip down the river that would normally take only twenty minutes had taken us almost two hours. I made a silent promise to avoid a repeat performance of such a nerve-racking experience. In future I would do my best to come into harbour in daylight.

Our peace was disturbed by a strange noise which at first I thought was another yacht approaching the holding pontoon. I rushed up to put fenders along *Lucia*'s starboard side, returned below and realised the noise was much louder inside *Lucia* than out. We eventually tracked it down to the electric water pump. As soon as I switched it off I lifted one of the access covers to the bilge, to discover it full of very hot water. I replaced the cover.

'To hell with it, Russ. I'll sort that problem out in the morning.'

Russel insisted we eat something before we fell into our bunks. He washed his hands once more before preparing a light meal, and explained that while he was trying to free *Lucia* from the mooring buoy he had felt something crawling over his hands. When he shone the torch on them, they were covered in revolting slimy insects. I'm glad he kept that gem of information to himself until we were safely in the marina. It doesn't do to send a stressed out skipper into hysterics.

CHAPTER FIVE

BILGES AND BOAT PEOPLE

We were woken up early the next morning by the marina staff, who had appointed *Lucia* a berth and wanted us to move into it as soon as possible. Once we had done so, I set about the task of investigating the problem with the water system. I eventually traced the fault to a split in one of the hoses. Because the gas water heater was on at the time the problem occurred, the lockers on the port side had been engulfed in steam. Now, having cooled down overnight, they were streaming with condensation and the bilges were full of fresh water.

Russel was very anxious to return to North Devon to see Rhiannon and asked if I objected to his father calling to collect him. The last thing I wanted was to have my ex-husband anywhere near me or *Lucia*, and immediately I began to feel under pressure. I explained my feelings to Russel, who agreed to meet him on neutral ground in the marina restaurant. But after they had spoken on the telephone Russ told me that there was something urgent his father needed to discuss with me – could he come to the boat to do so?

It may have been that I was still very tired from the voyage, but suddenly an overwhelming anxiety engulfed me. Russel tried to reassure me, saying that we would both meet his father at the restaurant and there was no need for him to come to the boat. He felt it was better for me to face my feelings rather than to hide from them, and promised that he would stay throughout the discussion.

When my ex-husband arrived I managed to control my nerves while Russel chatted to him about the trip for a short time, but then he said he would like to have a look at the boat. My heart leapt into my throat as I explained that that would not be possible. I gave him all sorts of reasons, but he refused to accept any of them. It is difficult to explain how, through continued badgering, this man felt sure he could get his own way. He had always done so, and I felt twenty-five years of unhappy marriage bearing down on me. The urgent matter he wanted to discuss could wait until he had seen the boat, he insisted.

Eventually Russel said that, if it was all right with me, he would take his father down and show him *Lucia* from the pontoon. Reluctantly I agreed. As I waited for them to return I had the feeling that the subject my ex-husband wanted to discuss with me would prove to be of little importance, and that the real purpose of his request to talk to me was to intrude into my new way of life. When they came back he was full of criticism. I cut him short and asked him to get to the point. His 'urgent matter' was so insignificant that I cannot even remember what the subject was. However, I can remember feeling totally defeated. Russ reminded his father that he wanted to get back to North Devon as quickly as possible, and to my relief they left.

LONE VOYAGER

Feeling emotionally drained, when I got back to *Lucia* I tried to sleep off my inner turmoil. I was woken up by the telephone ringing, and to my delight it was Paul's voice at the other end. After a long conversation with him, I felt a great deal better. He told me that he would be arriving the next evening to stay for a few days. With renewed energy I got on with sorting out *Lucia*, greatly intriguing the people on the next yacht. After watching me bale out bucket after bucket of water, my neighbours could not resist asking where it was all coming from. I explained to them what had happened with the split hose on the hot water system and then they asked me all sorts of questions about my future sailing plans.

As I lay in bed later that night thinking over recent events, the realisation that I had successfully completed my first voyage as skipper, without an experienced sailor aboard, caused a glow of pleasure to rise deep within me. I promised myself I would wait for the best possible conditions and then take *Lucia* out entirely alone to see how I fared.

By late afternoon next day *Lucia* was looking almost as good as new. I was making my way back to her after visiting the launderette when I bumped into the neighbours I had been talking to the previous day. They explained that they were returning home and were unlikely to see me again before I set sail for foreign parts. Wishing me luck, they handed me a gift-wrapped parcel. I asked them what I had done to deserve a present 'Keeping a smile on your face while baling out the bilges,' came the response. The parcel contained a green fluffy frog dressed in a souwester. The enclosed card informed me that her name was Mini Mo, that she never got seasick and could be relied on as a source of comfort when the going got tough. It was such a thoughtful thing to do that I resolved to write to them periodically throughout my future voyaging.

Paul and I had a wonderful time together catching up on lost time and planning my first single-handed voyage – direct to the island of Faial in the Azores, in the middle of the Atlantic. We made a long list of all the equipment to check, jobs to be completed and items to buy. Paul spent hours teaching me how to use my short-wave radio. Once I had set sail we planned to keep in daily radio contact, which was a great comfort to me. Knowing that we were going to be thousands of miles apart was going to be hard to endure; would our love survive such distance? Paul was confident it would and reassured me that, as he had by now launched his own yacht, *Faiz III*, it would not be long before he would be sailing in my wake.

I set myself many tasks to complete over the next few weeks. Each weekend Paul would arrive to check on my progress, and if possible we would set time aside to go sailing. Alternatively, we would just relax and enjoy each other's company. I also had to make time to visit as many of my family and friends as I could manage. This involved a great deal of travelling as Falmouth, situated at the southwest corner of England, is a long way from anywhere. I found these visits stressful but very worthwhile. I think I had my photograph taken more often than at any time in my life. Many of these people wanted to come and wave me goodbye, but I felt sure this would prove too emotional. The excuse I gave was that pinpointing the exact departure day in advance would be very difficult.

When I got back to Falmouth I was anxious to take *Lucia* out of the marina and sail her in the bay, completely alone. All that was required was for me to pluck up the necessary courage. Eventually I decided that, weather permitting, I would attempt this task the day after my birthday, as a very personal present to myself. I also decided it would be sensible to keep this plan a secret. The previous evening I went out for a birthday celebration with a group of friends. I had a great time, although I was careful not to over-indulge when the wine was being dispensed. I was not quite sure what I was going to encounter the next day but one thing I was sure of – a clear head would be an advantage.

The weather could not have been better, so there was nothing to prevent me from taking this giant leap. A friend of mine, Hywel, was working on his yacht which was moored in front of *Lucia*. He popped along for his usual early morning chat and, without me saying a word, understood what I was about to do.

'How long do you think you'll be out?'

'Probably four or five hours.'

'I'll be here to take your lines when you return,' he promised.

I checked *Lucia* over very carefully, hoping that I had done everything I could to make things run as smoothly as possible. Hywel helped me to cast off and, before I had a chance to add to my anxiety, I was motoring up the river towards St Anthony's Head.

During those few hours alone, I discovered many things about *Lucia* that had not been apparent before. There was a short, sharp chop to the sea and, no matter how hard I tried, I could not get her to tack to port. To begin with, each time she failed to respond I started the engine and motored her round. Then, with trial and error, I discovered that turning her completely around away from the wind did the trick. After I had done this several times, I pointed *Lucia* away from the land, sat in the cockpit and enjoyed my picnic lunch. I sat there indulging in the luxury of being totally alone, and felt confident that I would soon be ready to set sail for the Azores.

It was with some reluctance that I returned to the marina, though I was delighted to see Hywel and two other friends waiting for me on the pontoon. As soon as *Lucia* was secured I jumped ashore and hugged them all. Hywel confessed he had been very concerned about me and was pleased and relieved I had returned safely. I felt great. I had always known in my heart that I could sail *Lucia* alone, but proving it, if only for a few hours, had made me feel wonderful.

Later that evening, while I was talking to Paul on the phone, I casually said, 'I had lunch out today.'

'Oh, nice. Where did you go?'

'Just out in the bay on *Lucia*.'

'Great. Who came with you?'

'Nobody. It was just *Lucia* and me,' I giggled.

'Oh, Mo, that's wonderful! How was it?'

I spent several minutes going over the main points, and then went on to explain the difficulties I had experienced getting her to tack to port, and how I had eventually managed it.

'Ah, you mean you wore ship?'

'Well, I don't know about that. But after turning round so many times I certainly felt as if I was wearing her!'

Paul explained that this was an old nautical term, and that because of their design Sprays were known to be difficult to tack in a short, sharp sea.

'Great! Why on earth didn't you tell me this before?'

'Well, now you've not only found out for yourself, you've also discovered how to overcome it. Much more meaningful,' he assured me.

Over the next few days, any spare time I had was taken up with revising my astro navigation. It had been some time since my evening course and to begin with I was very rusty, but after referring to my old notes I soon began to regain my confidence. Although I had a GPS (global positioning system) that uses satellites to give you your longitude and latitude, I wanted to be sure that if necessary I could find my position using my sextant. In fact I planned to use both methods of navigation during my passage, so that I could check how accurate my astro navigation was.

I spent a whole day sorting out my charts, putting the ones I needed for the passage in the chart table and stowing the others in their locker. All my charts were second-hand, bought from a man whom Paul and I had met at a boat jumble. I had approximately 400 of them, purchased for 50p each. This was an amazing saving on the cost of £11 each for new charts. However, while I was sorting through them I decided to treat myself to a new chart of the Azores islands.

If weather conditions proved favourable, I planned to set off in early May. My sense of excitement was really heightened now. When Paul arrived to spend the weekend with me, I told him of my proposed leaving date. Our hearts soon became very heavy with the realisation that there were only a few more weekends left before we would be parted. Paul had brought me a great present, a very old copy of Joshua Slocum's book *Sailing Alone Around the World*, and had inscribed this message inside it: 'Well done on your first solo sail, may your pilot always guide you well, all my love, Paul.' Paul explained that I would understand the meaning of his inscription once I had read the book. Paul and Philip had told me a great deal about Captain Joshua Slocum, and although I tried to find time to dip into his book before I set sail for the Azores all I managed was the first few pages.

There were many reasons for making Faial my first port of call, the most important of which was the distance involved – some 1,100 miles. That would give me a passage of eleven to fourteen days in which to get used to *Lucia*. Also, a voyage of this distance would prove to me whether or not I was capable of single-handed sailing. Another good reason for choosing Faial stemmed from the fact that *Lucia* was a modern version of Joshua's yacht. As a result I had joined the Slocum Society, through which I had discovered that 20 July 1995 was the beginning of the centenary celebrations honouring Joshua's incredible circumnavigation. The island of Faial was Joshua's first port of call after leaving America, and the people of the Azores were organising special events to mark this occasion. Sprays from all over the world were planning to be in Faial for the festivities, and I was really looking forward to being one of them.

While I was in Falmouth I had met another single-handed sailor, William, who had recently sailed in from Holland on his beautiful yacht *Black Swan*. While admiring *Lucia* one day he enquired about the origin of her name. I explained that, about two years before *Lucia* was built, I was staying at a health clinic recovering from an illness. One of the other guests, Rodney Cattell insisted on calling me Lucy.

'My name is Mo,' I kept correcting him.

When he continued to refer to me as Lucy, I asked him why.

'I can see you have been very concerned about your illness – you may even have thought that you were going to die. But when I look at you I see no death, just a bright shining light coming from your eyes. Lucy is the English version of the Latin word for light,' he announced. I was quite astounded.

When I was searching for a name for my yacht, I phoned Rodney and asked him what the Latin version of Lucy was.

'Lucia,' he replied.

'That's it – that's the perfect name for my yacht. She is the light of my life and will be a beacon of light wherever I sail her.'

William agreed that it was a great name, and he felt certain she would live up to it.

During the following week I received a telephone call from my elder son, Colin.

'Mum, when are you planning to leave?'

'In about three weeks' time, darling.' There was a sharp intake of breath.

'Mum, I want to come and see you before you go.'

'I thought we'd already said our goodbyes. I know you're very busy at the moment, darling. Why don't you wait and come and have a wonderful holiday with me when I get to the Azores?'

'No, Mum, I want to come and see you once more before you leave. I'm very worried that you won't make it.'

I couldn't believe what he was saying to me – this was the first time I'd heard him react in this way.

'Come as soon as you can, darling. It will be wonderful to see you. I can understand you being concerned about me, but I promise you I have every intention of making it!'

This conversation left me feeling dreadful. How could I allay his fears? I had expected, once I had set sail, that my sons and the rest of my family and friends would feel a little concerned. However, that Colin thought I was going to die came as an unpleasant shock.

The following Sunday, after a great day's sailing I was returning to the marina with Paul and two other friends on board. Paul had gone forward to make the lines ready when he called back to me, saying that he thought Colin was standing at the fuel dock. We waved and yelled to him, indicating where we were going to berth, and he walked round to meet us. Fortunately I managed to make a very good entrance, bringing *Lucia* closely alongside the pontoon, so that all Paul had to do was step ashore and secure her.

Although Paul had not planned to leave until the next day, he decided to go that very evening so that Colin and I could spend some time alone. Once Paul and the others had left I started to talk to Colin about his anxieties.

'It's OK, Mum, now I'm here. Seeing you and the boat again. I feel a lot happier. Just promise me you'll be really, really careful.' I assured him I would not take any unnecessary risks and promised that I would always wear my harness when I left the cockpit. I could only deduce that his change of heart had come about as he watched me manoeuvre *Lucia* into harbour.

That evening I took Colin out to dinner at a place called Pandora's Inn, an ancient hostelry with a wonderful atmosphere and excellent food. Back on board *Lucia* we finished off some good wine, played cards and chatted happily until the early hours. When Colin left me the next morning, I felt sure he was a lot happier about my forthcoming voyage. I only hoped the feelings of doom and gloom would not return to him.

As ever, I started making lists of the items I would need to purchase before leaving. I was told by some of the people who had already visited the Azores that a lot of the everyday things we all take for granted were not available there. I was very lucky that so many of the friends I had made in Falmouth had cars and were happy to take me shopping. By the time I had completed my purchases you would have thought I was leaving the planet! Over a two-week period I laid in stores of everything from long life milk to all manner of tinned and packet foods, luxury biscuits, cakes, sweets and chocolate; six months' supply of shampoo, toilet paper, soap and toothpaste; all sorts of cosmetic items, from cotton wool to moisturiser; pens, pencils, blank recording tapes and batteries; engine spares, oil and distilled water. Finally, the day before I left, I shopped for all the fresh food items.

To accommodate the fruits of my mammoth shop I had to reorganise all the lockers and make a detailed record of what was where. It took more energy and time to complete this task than I had ever imagined it would. By the time I had stowed everything away I was really fed up – even the thought of going shopping made me want to scream.

I made more lists of things to do during the run-up to departure day. One of the most important tasks was a passage plan: this meant working out my route, then deciding how many miles to have between waypoints so that I could enter them into the GPS. I plotted the various courses to steer, how long it would take me to clear the shipping lanes and many other things that I hoped would help to make life easier for me once at sea.

By the end of the second week of May a strong south-westerly wind was well established. As this was the direction I would be sailing in, I had to delay my departure. I watched the weather very closely. What I really needed, to give myself the best possible start, was a forecast showing the winds coming from the north for at least three days. On 18 May, I got the forecast I was waiting for. I telephoned Paul and told him I planned to leave as close as possible to 10a.m. next day. He promised to be there at 9a.m. and, like it or not, he was bringing Russel, Philip and Denis with him. Denis was a dear man and a close friend of Paul's who had a short-wave radio. He had agreed to listen in during our radio schedules in case he had better contact with me, in which case he could relay messages between Paul and myself. When I protested that I would find it too upsetting if Russel was there, Paul told me Russel was determined to say a personal farewell to his Mum!

By mid-afternoon I was exhausted: I had done my fresh food shop and stowed it all away, I had cleaned *Lucia* throughout and double-checked my passage plan.

Since I had promised to meet some of the friends I had made in Falmouth at the marina restaurant that evening for a farewell meal, I thought I would have a little nap to regain some energy for later. Then I phoned as many of my family and friends as I could before my emotions got the better of me. It was my call to Sheila, my youngest sister, that finally did it.

'You don't really want to go, do you?' she sobbed.

'Yes, of course I do.'

'Then why are you crying?'

'Because *you* are.'

'Mo, promise me you're doing this for you – that you're not just doing it because you feel under pressure, having said you'll do it.'

'I promise, I promise. Please try not to worry, darling. I'll phone you when I get to the Azores.'

After that I felt unable to phone my best girlfriend, Jo, as just the sound of her voice would have had me totally awash again. I decided to leave that phone call until later in the evening, when I hoped I would be more in control.

I had a long hot shower, and while I was washing my hair I wondered how long it would be before I enjoyed this wonderful pleasure again. By this time I was running late – when I joined my friends in the restaurant I was unfortunately too late for a meal and had to make do with a sandwich. People I hardly knew were coming up to me, shaking my hand and wishing me luck. While I was chatting to one man who had just returned from a long ocean passage he suddenly disappeared, only to return with a good luck charm in the shape of a brightly coloured fish head with a smaller fish hanging from its mouth. As he handed it to me, he explained that some friends he had made on a Pacific island had given it to him. He had great faith in it, and was sure that if I hung it in my cabin it would also serve me well.

Truly touched by his kind thought and generosity, I asked, 'Are you sure you wouldn't rather keep it for your next voyage?'

'No, I'd be very happy if you would accept it – I think you will need it more than me.'

I was not really too sure how to take this but, never being one to turn away luck, I thanked him and promised I would hang it up in my cabin. As I returned to *Lucia* that night, my ears were ringing with the good wishes of so many people.

Before going to bed I phoned my dear friend Jo and told her that, God willing, I would be leaving in the morning. I asked if she would just put down the phone when we had finished talking, knowing that to say goodbye would start me crying again. We chatted for a while and I gave her Paul's telephone number, explaining that if we were successful in our radio contact he would happily pass on news of my progress to my family and friends. I promised I would contact her on my arrival in the Azores. She told me to be very careful and that she loved me dearly – and suddenly the line went dead. As I replaced the receiver the tears were streaming down my face.

CHAPTER SIX

FALMOUTH TOWARDS THE AZORES

When I awoke at 5a.m. I was amazed that I had managed to sleep so soundly. I looked out to check the direction of the wind: it was from the west. Well, that was OK – it was forecast to go north-west. I just hoped the meteorologists were right. That morning, as I washed and dressed, I tried to think serene thoughts.

I prepared my sea berth in the main saloon and put at one end all the clothes I thought I would need for the first few days of the voyage. In a waterproof bag I placed gloves, scarf, torch, spare batteries and kitchen timer. Along with my harness, I stowed these items in the cockpit. Then I started in the forward cabin, working my way to the stern, checking that everything was secure. I made repeated visits to the heads, always a sure sign that I was feeling anything but calm. I heated some milk and ate a bowl of warm Weetabix in the hope that it would soothe my churning stomach, but to no avail. I went on deck, removed the sail cover and collected all the loose items to stow them safely below.

I was halfway through preparing my picnic when I heard somebody calling me from the pontoon. I popped my head out and could hardly believe my eyes – my sister Sheila and her husband Stuart were smiling down at me. They had travelled by train overnight to see me before I left. What a wonderful surprise! Sheila explained that she could not let me go without hugging me, no matter how upsetting she found it. She has a bone-wasting condition that causes her dreadful pain and a long train journey would have been quite an ordeal for her. It was a sacrifice that I appreciated immensely, and within seconds we were crying and laughing at the same time. I made them tea and talked to them while I got on with preparing my picnic, which I put in the cockpit along with my navigational instruments. Having these items handy in the cockpit, I explained to Sheila and Stuart, would save me having to go below for a few hours, which hopefully would prevent me from getting seasick.

I was back on deck, hanking on my storm jib to the baby stay in preparation for conditions that I hoped I would not encounter, when I saw Russel, Paul and the others making their way towards me. More hugs, kisses and tears. Sheila stepped into the role of galley slave, producing endless cups of tea and coffee for my ever-increasing farewell committee. Bless her, she cleared everything up, so all I had to do was stow it where it belonged. I had to keep apologising for my frequent visits to the heads. Paul helped me check that all was ready on deck. Both he and Philip said how impressed they were to see me so well organised.

He looked at his watch. 'It's almost time, Mo. Best to start saying your farewells.'

I swallowed hard and went below. Everybody wanted to take photos and then, before I knew it, I was hugging and kissing them one by one as they made their way ashore.

Russel made me laugh when he said he could not understand why so many people were crying on such a great day. He gave me a really big hug and made me promise to be very careful. By the time I passed to Sheila neither of us could say a word; we just kissed each other. I watched with very tearful eyes as Russel helped her up the companionway steps.

Paul took me in his arms, and as he kissed me I realised his face was very wet. When I opened my eyes to look at him. I was amazed to see this huge man with tears pouring down his cheeks. We had arranged to meet in Lisbon in September and I tried to comfort him by saying, 'Keep looking forward to September.'

He kissed me, gently wiped my own tears away and said, 'I'll rig up some lines and take them on to the adjoining boat to make it easier for you to leave the pontoon.'

I asked him to hold me very tight just for a few seconds. Neither of us spoke. We didn't need to – there was so much love encompassed in that embrace.

Up in the fore-cabin I washed my face, took some very deep breaths, changed into my thermal sailing kit, clipped my peaked cap securely on my head and took one last look around the interior of *Lucia* before stepping out into the cockpit. Paul was now busy with the lines and I started the engine. I took another look around the deck. Everything appeared to be satisfactory. Philip, holding his hand-held VHF radio, said they were all going up to Pendennis Point to watch me pass by and would call me on the radio as I did so. I gestured to Paul that I was ready, and turned towards the host of tear-stained, smiling faces on the pontoon. Sheila and Stuart were holding up a huge banner reading: 'BON VOYAGE MO WE ALL LOVE YOU.' I called to them to throw it to me, caught it and tossed it down below. Then I put the engine in gear as Paul and Denis threw my lines aboard

Lucia and we gently motored away. As I turned round once more to wave to the cheering crowd, a strange, dream-like feeling engulfed me. Was this really happening, or was it just a figment of my vivid imagination?

I switched the electronic self-steering on and went forward to collect the discarded mooring lines and the now redundant fenders. When I reached the mouth of the river I turned *Lucia* into the wind and raised the main sail. I unfurled the jib and pointed *Lucia* towards the sea. As we passed St Anthony's Head I trimmed the sails, and when I felt *Lucia* lift her petticoats as the wind filled her sails I turned the engine off.

As I came level with Pendennis Point, Philip called me on the VHF radio.

'*Lucia* looks beautiful. You've got her sailing really well. How do you feel, Mo?'

'Thanks. I made sure her make-up was just perfect before we left,' I giggled. 'I feel fine, Phil. A bit hot with all the effort but happy that everything seems to be working well. I'm going to give the coastguard a call and then I'll get back to you.' ...

'Falmouth coastguard, Falmouth coastguard. This is the yacht *Lucia*, *Lucia*. Over.'

'*Lucia*, *Lucia*. Falmouth coastguard. Go to channel 67.'

'Channel 67.' I switched channels and waited for them to call me.

'*Lucia*, *Lucia*. Falmouth coastguard. Over.'

'Falmouth coastguard, this is *Lucia*. I have just left the Falmouth Yacht Marina, bound for the island of Faial in the Azores, ETA fourteen days. Over.'

'*Lucia*, please describe your vessel and how many people you have on board. Over.'

'Falmouth coastguard, *Lucia* is a thirty-three-foot, white steel Spray with a black stripe. I am sailing single-handed so there are no other people on board. Over.'

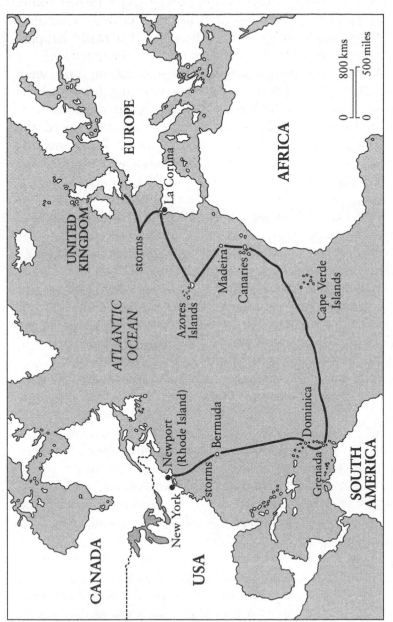

Mo's voyages in *Lucia*

'*Lucia, Lucia*. Thank you for that information. Have a pleasant and safe voyage. Over.'

'Falmouth coastguard, thank you very much. I'm sure I will. *Lucia* out.'

Giving this report to the coastguard suddenly brought the realisation home to me. This was what *Lucia* had been created for – I was actually doing what I had dreamed of for so long. *Lucia* and I were on our way. As I looked behind to see us slipping away from St Anthony's Head, I let out a huge whoop of delight.

I called Philip on the VHF, but it was Paul who responded.

'You look and sound great. How are you feeling? Over.'

'Wonderful, Paul. After all this time we're finally on our way. I'm so excited. Is Russel there? Over.'

'Hi, Mum. It looks amazing seeing you disappearing out to sea. Over.'

'It *feels* amazing, darling. You take good care of yourself and don't ever forget how much I love you. Is Auntie Sheila still with you? Over.'

'Hi, Mo. I wouldn't have missed this for all the world. Just promise me once more that you'll be careful.'

'I promise, darling. Sheila, thank you so much for making that wonderful banner, I'll treasure it forever. Can I have another word with Paul, please? Over.'

There was silence for a few moments, and then I heard Philip's voice.

'Paul's a bit tied up at the moment, but he said to tell you he'll talk to you tonight on the short-wave radio as arranged. Over.'

'Oh, OK, Phil. Is everything all right? Over.'

'Yes, fine, dear. Now we'd better make this the last transmission because you're almost out of range. Over.'

'Philip, I'd just like you to know that without you and

Paul – especially Paul – this day would never have dawned. I will never be able to thank both of you enough. Over.'

When Philip responded I could hear the emotion in his voice.

'Thank you, dear. I'll pass that message on to Paul. Fair winds and safe voyage. Over.'

'God bless you all, and thank you so much for giving me such a wonderful send-off. *Lucia* out.'

Looking back towards the land, wondering if they could still see *Lucia*, I silently thanked them once more and told them how much I loved them all.

As we progressed, I entered the relevant data into my log. The wind was still coming from the west and *Lucia* and I were sailing along beautifully, doing a very respectable speed of just over five knots.

I had no idea what lay ahead, but I promised *Lucia* that somehow I would find the strength to cope. Now I had to try and relax to conserve my energy. I had a good look round, checked my watch and then got comfortable in the cockpit. It was wonderful sitting there watching the land disappear, with nobody to interrupt my thoughts.

However I had a strong desire to get up and check we were still clear of other vessels, though when I looked at my watch, I found I had only been sitting down for eight minutes. I was trying to train myself to look around every fifteen. But it was no good – I just could not sit still. I had to have another look around, just to put my mind at rest. All clear! I plotted my position on the chart. Soon I would be reaching the point when I would have to alter course. Then I would turn the electronic autopilot off and try to set my wind vane self-steering to keep us on course. After another quick look round I sat down and ate a little of my picnic.

After changing course, trimming the sails and setting

up the wind vane I felt quite tired. I set my kitchen timer for fifteen minutes and tried to doze. A moment of disquiet entered my head; what would it be like watching the sun go down, knowing that I was facing my first night completely alone at sea? Fear began to creep into my stomach, but I quickly pushed it away. I listened to *The Archers* on Radio 4 and then recorded the shipping forecast. The wind was going to continue from the west but drop in strength. Maybe it would go more northerly tomorrow. I was feeling very tired now and did my best to snooze between keeping watch. I was surprised that each time I woke up a few minutes before the alarm went off. I continued to nibble at my picnic throughout the afternoon, even though I did not feel in the least bit hungry.

By now, due to the light wind and the direction of the tide, *Lucia* and I were motor sailing. I wanted to try and keep our speed at four knots, to clear the shipping lanes within the first thirty-six hours. So far the traffic had been relatively light, but the sooner we were out of the shipping lanes the happier I would be. It was getting quite chilly, so I went below and collected more clothes, along with my sleeping bag and pillow. Before I left I had made up my mind that I would spend the first few nights in the cockpit. I felt it was easier on my mind to do so, no matter how cold it was. As I looked at my watch I realised it would not be long before my first radio sked with Paul, and the feeling of excitement made me tingle all over. I hoped to goodness that we would be able to make contact.

As the sun dipped below the horizon my heart went with it, for night would very soon be upon me. I tried to concentrate on the joy I had always felt during the nights when others were on board with me, but I still felt a little afraid So I kept myself busy. Clipping my harness to the lifeline I made my way forward, checking that all was as it should be. Once back in the cockpit I turned the engine off for a while, hoping the wind alone would keep our speed up. My fear was at its height during twilight, but once night had properly descended the more I gazed at the starlit sky the better I felt.

A few minutes before the appointed hour I went below and tuned in the radio; one last check outside and then back down to the radio. As I depressed the button on the mike, my heart was beating really fast.

'*Faiz III, Faiz III*, this is *Lucia, Lucia*. Over.'

'*Lucia, Lucia*, this is *Faiz III*. How're you doing, Mo? Over.'

'Just great, Paul. It's so wonderful to hear your voice. Over'.

'It's great to hear yours, too. Give me your position, Mo. Over.'

I gave Paul my latitude and longitude, the course I was steering, the wind direction and the speed we were making. We chatted backwards and forwards for ten minutes, and then I asked him to stand by while I went up on deck to have a good look round.

'Paul, there are lights on the horizon so I'll have to go soon. Over.'

'OK, Denis is also on frequency. See if you can pick him up. Over.'

I called Denis but I could not receive him as well as Paul, so we just had a few words and then I returned to Paul.

'Mo, be careful and try and get some rest tonight. Make sure you don't let yourself get too cold. I'll talk to you in the morning. Over.'

'I'll do my best, Paul. Don't worry about me. 88s, 88s,' I said, using the radio jargon for love and kisses. 'I hope I'll be able to get through in the morning. Over.'

'OK, if you can't get through do as we arranged, give your position to the UK Maritime Net. 88s, 88s. Take care. *Faiz III* going clear.'

'All understood, Paul. Sleep well, my love. 88s, 88s. *Lucia* out.'

I rushed into the cockpit. The lights of the other vessel were closer, but still far enough away not to be a problem. I watched it pass a good way in front of me as it made its way up the English Channel. I saw many lights that night and, although I was very tired, I found it very difficult to sleep even for fifteen minutes or less at a time. The thought of being run down by another vessel is a very effective way of keeping watch. To my surprise, the hours of darkness passed extremely quickly. As I watched the new day dawning I felt so happy that, despite the danger of other vessels, bad weather and the all-too-likely prospect of seasickness, at last I was doing what I really wanted to do.

I ate a little more of my picnic and after a short time, with renewed energy, I went below to clean my teeth and wash my face. I felt a little unwell and was glad to return to the cockpit, where I snuggled down into my sleeping bag and dozed for a short time. I called Paul as arranged, but conditions were not quite as good as the night before. So after giving him my position and bucket-loads of 88s I returned to my sleeping bag, still feeling a little queasy.

At 8.30a.m. I plotted my position on the chart and was disappointed to discover I had not made the progress I had hoped for. The wind had gone round to the north-west but it was very light. I started the engine and we motor sailed for several hours. Two other ships passed us quite close during the morning and through binoculars I could see the name of one of them, *Sea Trade*. I wondered where they were bound and what their cargo was.

By early afternoon the wind had gone very light, so I furled my working jib and unfurled my light weather genoa. As we picked up speed I turned the engine off, and the peace was wonderful! Unfortunately I paid homage to Neptune very soon afterwards and, although it was the last thing I wanted to do, I nibbled on digestive biscuits in the hope that I could replenish my stomach. The wind had died completely by 5.30p.m. and we had to resume motor sailing well into the night.

I was nowhere near as worried when darkness fell on that second night. It felt a great deal colder, though, and immediately I had recovered from being sick yet again I went below and filled a hot water bottle. Before long, it was time to call Paul. Conditions were much better at night but being down below made my sickness worse, so I had to cut our conversation short and that made me very cross with myself. Keeping watch that second night was no problem. When my head was not up looking around it was over the side, feeding the meagre contents of my stomach to the fish.

The dreadful seasickness continued for four days and I was becoming very weak. The wind had changed to the south-west and picked up to a force four to five. Pounding hard to windward, the motion of *Lucia* was far from comfortable. During those four days I had tried most of the seasick remedies I had on board, but to no avail; I was unable to keep anything down. There was just one method left to try: Carol Farmer, an American friend I had made in Falmouth, had given me two Phenergan suppositories, but they were very strong and Carol had warned me that they could make me drowsy.

I had no choice – it was dangerous to let my condition deteriorate further. I was well out of the shipping lanes and I had not seen another vessel for days. After speaking to Paul that morning I checked all was well with *Lucia*, lay down below in my sea berth and administered the first suppository. Two hours later I awoke, dragged myself up to the cockpit and had a good look around. I felt reassured to find an empty sea. I checked my course and staggered back to my bunk for another two hours. When I surfaced for the second time, I felt like a new woman. I'm sure it was a two-fold solution; first, and most importantly, the Phenergan had stopped the seasickness; secondly, I had had the longest sleep since leaving Falmouth. Once I was reassured that *Lucia* was sailing along quite happily, I sat in the cockpit and wrapped my sleeping bag around me. I sipped some water, rested and was soon back to my routine of keeping watch every fifteen to twenty minutes.

Six hours after administering the first suppository, I was faced with a dilemma. Should I use the last of the medication, or save it for future use? I weighed up the pros and cons and decided to use it. I felt it was wiser to be sure that I had banished the dreaded SS completely, and then I could work on rebuilding my strength. This time, with the aid of my alarm I managed to wake every twenty minutes. During my awake periods, I ate digestive biscuits and drank mineral water. By nightfall I was feeling a great deal better. When I spoke to Paul that evening he was extremely relieved to hear that I had put the fish on a diet.

The next day the south-westerly wind was very lively, and even with a reefed mainsail we were doing between five and six knots. Conditions were well and truly keeping me on my toes. I was either leaping around the deck releasing sheets that kept getting caught around every available object, or holding on to the grab bar above the companionway in the cockpit and singing at the top of my voice. I felt wonderful, probably due to the fact that I had been eating very well, albeit in the most unlady-like fashion – straight from the pan in which I had cooked the food. I had even managed to eat dessert for the first time since setting sail.

By late afternoon I had deep reefed the main sail and raised the storm jib to make life as comfortable as possible. That night the sea was an amazing sight – a mass of white horses and full of phosphorescence. I sat as snug as I could in the cockpit, enjoying the spectacle until the weather deteriorated and it started to rain heavily. After convincing myself that we were under control, that Joshua (my wind vane self-steering) was coping and there was nothing further I could do, I went below, shutting the cockpit door behind me. I lay in my warm, dry bunk, listening to the waves crashing into *Lucia* and only venturing into the cockpit every twenty minutes to check all was well.

At daybreak the wind had reduced in strength, so I reset the sails to full main and working jib. I plotted my position, to discover I had made good only half the distance I had hoped for – we still had just over 840 miles to go. I reminded myself that it did not matter how long it took me to get to the Azores as I needed the experience of a long passage.

During my next conversation with Paul, because of the south-westerly he advised me to consider the easier route via northern Spain. However, my determination to continue directly to the Azores was as strong as ever. As I sat in the cockpit, amazed at the calming influence the angry ocean was having on me, I contemplated what I should do with my free time that day. I decided to have my first strip wash; when I was land-based I was used to at least one shower or bath each day. At sea, so far I had only managed a daily face wash and a quick clean of the teeth. I ate a bar of chocolate to give myself an extra burst of energy, went below and, hanging on with one hand, washed myself all over with the other. Once the task was completed, I was exhausted and had to lie down to recuperate.

Smelling extremely sweet and feeling absolutely wonderful in my clean thermal underwear, I went topsides to check all was still well. Looking forward, I saw that the bulk of the furling genoa sheet, which I had neatly curled and tied to the pulpit, was trailing in the water. Without a single thought for my clean, dry clothes I put on my harness and went to the bowsprit to retrieve the wayward sheet. At that moment, *Lucia* dipped her bows and I took several waves over the lower part of my body. I secured the sheet and returned below soaking wet, none too pleased with myself. I felt angry that I had not had the common sense to put on my foul weather gear before undertaking such a task. I had no choice but to revert to my smelly long-johns until the other pair were dry. It seemed I was only capable of learning the hard way!

Later that day I tried to toast some bread under the grill. Although the cooker was gimballed, *Lucia*'s lively motion made the grill pan keep leaping off the shelf. At the risk of burning my fingers I knelt down on the floor and held the pan in place. As I munched my hard-earned toast I felt very tired and fed up with bashing to windward. By early evening I had changed course and was heading south – enough was enough. I would sail down the Spanish and Portuguese coast until I could turn west towards the Azores. From now on I would go with the wind instead of into it.

By the next day we were sailing along reasonably smoothly, doing between four and five knots, with the wind from the west. I had spoken to Paul again; this time conditions were excellent and we chatted for about thirty minutes. There was, however, a sting in the tail: Paul told me a series of lows were predicted to pass over Britain during the next few days bringing strong winds and heavy rain. When I listened to the BBC shipping forecast at midday it spoke of winds increasing to force seven. As the sea was already kicking up, I decided to set the storm jib and deep reef the main.

This time the BBC was not wrong. Before long –

while I was below, of course, helping myself to a longed for orange – the wind shifted remarkably quickly and all hell broke loose topsides. *Lucia* was hove-to; it was all hands on deck. After a while this single pair of hands managed to get things straight. In such a sea *Lucia* would not tack, so I had to wear ship. This required putting Lucia on to the other tack by turning her away from the wind, jibing her round. I was beginning to get used to this manoeuvre but it was very unnerving in such a steep sea.

That evening the wind became even stronger. As I had already prepared *Lucia* to the best of my ability, I decided to sit in the cockpit and try to relax. On the starboard side, far on the horizon, I saw a line squall. I had never seen one at sea before but there was no mistaking it. I had that mainsail down in a flash, hardened in the storm jib, hung on and waited. I was mesmerised by the spectacular sight. The squall came towards us as if someone was pushing a huge, charcoal-coloured curtain. The wind was whipping up the sea before it and the rain was relentlessly pounding down. When it hit *Lucia* she was well ready for it and there was no real problem – she rode the waves very well. After a short time it passed over and I watched until it had disappeared.

I raised the deep reefed main, reset the storm jib and settled down once more to try and relax. As darkness descended I began to feel really cold. I went below to get warm, feeling reasonably content and believing *Lucia* was as ready as she could be to weather whatever the elements might throw at us. Oh, how easy it is to fool a novice sailor!

When the terrible storm that turned my headsail into a dangerous, wind-filled balloon shattered my sleep at 3 a.m., I had no comprehension of what I was about to endure. As reality continued to slap me in the face with a vengeance, I struggled with the hard fact that although I had done all I could it was in vain. Even the small comfort I had derived from eventually making contact with Paul, and agreeing with him that I should now call off in northern Spain instead of going direct to the Azores, was diminished as the storm raged on.

I had been dragging myself out of my bunk every fifteen to twenty minutes to keep watch and plot my position. By now my continued seasickness had made me very weak. I was badly dehydrated, and when I went to the heads and saw how dark my urine was I knew I just had to do something to stop being sick. But since I had used the last of the Phenergan I had no other way to achieve this than sheer willpower. I sat down and tried to pinpoint my anxiety. With *Lucia*'s rig vibrating so violently, my main fear was focused on the fact that I was sure the rigging would fail and the mast would fall down.

I put my harness on and ventured out into the cockpit. The force of the gale was unbelievable, and the wind screamed through the rigging as horizontal driving rain blinded me. Waves were continually washing over the deck as *Lucia* rushed along at a terrifying speed. The motion was incredible as she corkscrewed through the waves, violently rolling and pitching as the pounding seas hit her. Despite this, I felt it was imperative to find out how the rig was faring.

I went out on to the deck, clinging to every available handhold. Slipping and sliding as the waves washed over me, half on my bottom and half crawling, I shuffled, along the side decks in order to check the rigging. To my amazement each part felt as solid as a rock. It was then that I knew if *Lucia* could take such a hammering without sustaining any more damage, she would survive. My body, on the other hand, was in grave danger of losing the battle!

Once I was back in the cockpit I gave myself a strong talking to, trying to convince myself that it was essential to conquer the seasickness. From that moment on my determination to survive took over, and by the third day of the storm I was able to keep a little water down. Later that day the balloon in the fore sail started to split, relieving the pressure on the rig, and the vibration began to lesson. This helped my frame of mind greatly. In addition, with *Lucia*'s motion now a little more comfortable I began to feel somewhat better.

By now I was extremely busy, constantly correcting my course due to the wind and current pushing me too far north-east. Happily, by early evening, even with the erratic behaviour of the by now torn and tattered genoa we were making reasonable progress. Paul had managed to borrow a radio from a friend, but due to poor contact we had only been able to relay messages via a third party. That night, however, conditions were greatly improved and I was able to have a long talk with him direct. He was very concerned about me, and I did my best to allay his fears by reassuring him that life might not be perfect but my spirits were in good shape. I told him of my decision to do away with the furling genoa system and replace it with a hank on sail. He promised he would organise Chris Skanes, the sailmaker, to make me a new sail which he would somehow get to me, along with the other items I needed, as quickly as possible. Then, once I had made the necessary repairs, I could continue my voyage to the Azores. All I had to do was get *Lucia* and myself safely into harbour.

By early next morning, thirty miles from La Coruna, the weather had greatly improved and things were looking much better. Then ahead of me I spotted several fishing vessels. I had to manoeuvre *Lucia* through what appeared to be the complete Spanish fishing fleet; there were boats everywhere. One of them circled me three times. I waved and smiled, then called them on the VHF, but received no response. They just circled me closer until I could almost see the whites of their eyes. I began to feel very uneasy. What was their problem? Why would they not talk to me on the radio or wave at me? After a while they took off. Who could blame them? What self-respecting Spanish fishermen would want to talk to a near-skeleton of a woman, with a headsail in tatters, flying the red ensign?

Land, yes, yes! There it was, looking for all the world like a low grey cloud. When it continued to stay at the same spot on the horizon, growing taller, I knew that after eleven days at sea my navigation had not let me down. I went below and got my Radio Direction Finder. I had never used it at sea before, but as I had no detailed charts of this area the RDF was the only way I had of being sure that the land I was approaching was La Coruna.

I looked in the pilot book to discover what letters I should listen for in Morse code, put on the earphones and swung the instrument slowly from starboard to port. Hearing nothing, I reread the details in the book and found that I was only just in range of the beacon. I continued on my course and patiently waited until we had progressed a few miles further towards the land.

My doubts mounting, I tried again, slowly swinging the RDF from side to side. It gave me such a shock when I heard the Morse – I became so excited I just could not work out what the sounds represented. I had to listen for a long time before I was sure I had interpreted it correctly, but it was definitely the radio beacon at La Coruna. I remembered what Paul had said to me: 'On a steel boat you must line the RDF up over the ship's compass. As you slowly swing the instrument, you will hear the Morse. As it fades to silence and then comes clear again, you must note the bearing when you can't hear the signal – that is the direction of the beacon.'

I put *Lucia* on course and watched as the land became clearer. I felt so excited that I went below for my camera and took far too many photos. Then I began to prepare *Lucia* for harbour. Mooring lines port and starboard on the centre cleats, the same on the stern and a bowline. Back to the cockpit to check on the course and to rest for a short time. As I was approaching what I hoped would be the harbour, I dropped the mainsail and tied it as carefully as I could.

A fishing boat was coming up fast behind me. At first I felt frightened – what if the skipper had not seen me? To be hit by another vessel so close to the harbour and safety would be truly tragic. I returned to the helm and stood by to change course if necessary. Thankfully, the boat passed me with ample room on my starboard side. I watched the fishing boat carefully. Surely it must be heading for the same place as me, but it was moving so fast that there was no way I could keep up with it. As I sat down in the cockpit all the strength seemed to evaporate from my body. I realised that because I was so exhausted I was having irrational thoughts. I rested for a short time and then tried to think clearly, realising that I must do only what was absolutely necessary, slowly and carefully, in order to conserve as much energy as possible. Once more I studied the plan of the harbour in the Cruising Association book, and told myself that it looked quite straightforward. All I had to do was stay calm and all would be well.

I heard someone calling La Coruna Radio on the VHF, and they responded in English. Great – what had I got to lose? I called them and changed to the channel they requested. I told them I had a problem with my rig and that I needed to come alongside a pontoon in the marina to make repairs. They instructed me to call the marina on another channel. I then explained that I was single-handed and wondered if it was possible to arrange for some help with my lines. The radio operator immediately came back and asked me to stand by. Within a few minutes he returned to tell me that he had contacted the marina and a berth would be waiting for me, together with some people who would take my lines. What an angel! My energy seemed to return and I continued to prepare *Lucia*.

I went up to the bows, grabbed handfuls of the tattered headsail and tied it to the pulpit. The last thing I needed was for the wayward sail to obscure my vision. Then I put fenders on both sides of *Lucia*. All I had to do now was make a safe entry into the harbour and then the marina berth. Someone was calling *Lucia* on the VHF radio. A British yacht that was not very far from me had heard my conversation with La Coruna Radio and offered to show me the way in. By then I could clearly see the harbour mole but I accepted their offer, as I had no idea what to expect once I had rounded the wall.

All of a sudden a very fast motor launch came straight towards me – I was stunned at its speed. It was the police, who were pointing at my stern and yelling something I could not understand. Oh, my God, they want to board me, I thought!

I could not have been more wrong. Somehow they had spotted the safety line that connects the self-steering rudder to the stern rail, and thought it was in danger of fouling the propeller. I explained that it was OK and thanked them for their concern. They wished me well and sped away as fast as they had appeared. Life was beginning to feel surreal – everybody was being so kind to me.

As I rounded the harbour mole, I was shocked to see so many other vessels. I carefully followed the British

yacht, and Susan, the skipper's wife, called me again on
the VHF and directed me to the marina. Then they
altered course to pick up a mooring. Susan said that as
soon as they were able they would launch their dinghy
and come to assist me. I thanked her, but said I was
sure it would not be necessary.

I had to concentrate very hard as I manoeuvred *Lucia*
through the other yachts. It was very difficult as the
wind was blowing quite hard, catching the remains of
the damaged headsail and continually blowing her bows
off. The marina pontoons became visible and I saw three
people waving at me. I slowly approached them, constantly correcting *Lucia*'s heading. When I felt I had
lined her up as best as I could, I went along the side
deck to the centre cleat and threw my line as hard as
possible. One of the men caught it and another yelled
for the bowline. He missed it! Quickly I retrieved the
line from the water, but by then *Lucia*'s bows were
being blown off. As she started to swing round I rushed
to the stern and threw that line. It was caught, and the
men managed to start to pull *Lucia* towards the pontoon.
I went forward and threw the bowline to the third man,
and within a few minutes *Lucia* was secured to the
pontoon.

Those three wonderful men – Dutch, as it turned out
– immediately came aboard. One of their number
climbed the mast and between them they removed the
damaged sail. I thanked them with all my heart. At last
Lucia and I were safe.

CHAPTER SEVEN

BACK ON TERRA FIRMA

It was not quite the entrance into my first port of call I had hoped for, or indeed dreamt of, but I still felt exhilarated. Apart from the storm-damaged sail there were very few visible signs of my dramatic first solo voyage. I went below and called Russell Cob, the American sailor and radio ham who was relaying messages to Paul. After congratulating me he said he was greatly relieved, and confessed that from his first contact with me he had been extremely concerned. He advised me to have a good rest and enjoy myself in La Coruna, which he assured me was a wonderful place to have made landfall.

I was trying to tidy up the cockpit, but my eyes kept wandering all around the marina. I found it difficult to believe that I had really arrived. There were several people taking a great interest in *Lucia*; I smiled at them all – in fact I just could not stop smiling. I saw a man rushing along the pontoon making directly for *Lucia* and for a moment I thought I recognised him. But then I dismissed the idea – I could not possibly know anybody here.

He stood looking at me for a moment and then said, 'Mo, I knew it was you. There couldn't possibly be two yachts like *Lucia*.'

It was Geoff Trott, a sailing instructor I had met in Falmouth. He was in La Coruna as tutor to a crew of English men on their motor sailing yacht *Tribute*, which was moored at the far end of the harbour. Geoff and the rest of the crew had watched *Lucia*'s entrance. I invited him aboard and he immediately asked what he could do to help.

I was so surprised to meet somebody I knew that for a while I could not think straight. We sat in the cockpit and, as I described my voyage and the storm we had just weathered a look of concern entered his eyes.

'Why don't you just collect your wash kit together and I'll walk with you to the shower unit? I'll wait in the bar so I can buy you a drink afterwards,' he offered.

He couldn't have come up with a better suggestion – a shower was something I really needed.

'Will *Lucia* be all right? Shouldn't I stay on board for a little longer to make sure she's safe?' I asked.

He smiled at me and said she would be just fine.

As I gingerly stepped ashore a great rush of fatigue washed over me. Geoff took my arm and very slowly we walked along the pontoon towards the yacht club. Everything felt so strange. As Geoff directed me to the shower block, my mind wandered back to the last shower I had had in Falmouth. So much had happened since then. Before setting sail, I had never envisaged that my voyage would be easy. However, I had also never imagined that my learning curve would be quite so steep!

I undressed and looked at myself in the mirror, I had certainly lost weight – in fact I looked positively skinny. I stepped into the shower, turned on the water and it promptly knocked me over. I sat there for a few seconds and then slowly got up, supporting myself on the walls. I knew I was weak, but up until that moment I had not realised just how weak.

When I arrived in the bar, feeling extremely clean but very tired, my first thought was to make my apologies to Geoff and return to *Lucia* to sleep for a year. He would have none of it.

'What you need, my girl, is some food,' he urged.

I could not argue with that. I had been dreaming for days that, when I got into harbour, my first meal would be Dover sole, new potatoes and salad. Miracle of miracles, apart from having French fries instead of new potatoes that was what I had. Geoff was still insisting on buying me a celebration drink. After some resistance I agreed to have a glass of white wine, which I sipped as I ate my meal. Unfortunately, although my mind desperately wanted to eat every last morsel, my stomach could only tolerate a small amount. Geoff left me in peace to eat and went to join some friends in another part of the bar. While I was toying with my food, I watched more people begin to gather. As their conversations began to rise in volume, I thought how strange it all sounded. For the past eleven days, I had not seen a single human being, and now I was surrounded by them. I began to eavesdrop; their laughter was pure joy to hear.

Suddenly I felt very anxious to telephone my family and friends, but as I had no Spanish money I was not sure how I could achieve this. Geoff had already offered to lend me the cost of my meal; I wondered if I could be cheeky enough to ask him for some extra to make my calls. I went and stood beside him, waiting for a break in the conversation. But as soon as he saw me he started to introduce me to so many other people that my head began to spin. One after the other they warmly shook my hand as they fired questions at me.

'Did you really sail here alone? Surely it's impossible for such a little woman to have done such a thing?' one of the guys asked. I hardly got a chance to answer one person before another one was interrupting – they were all eager to know what had happened on my voyage.

I quickly realised that I was not up to such a deluge of questions, so I just stood there smiling, waiting for them to run out of steam. Then I gave them all the same answer.

'I'm very lucky that *Lucia*'s a strong yacht and she's extremely forgiving of my many mistakes. All I really had to do was stay calm – I knew all would turn out well in the end.'

Some of them shook their heads; others gave me what I took to be knowing smiles. It was not until many weeks later that I was to learn what a few of them were really thinking!

Geoff was only too pleased to extend my loan and I phoned as many of my family and friends as I could. All of them were delighted and relieved to hear from me. Colin wanted to send me flowers; after his original fears for my safety he was so glad I had arrived safely in port.

Russel was temporarily living at the house I had once shared with his father, and I hoped that he would be the one to answer the phone. Unfortunately it was my ex-husband.

'Give me your number and I'll get him to call you back,' he said. I failed to recognise the trap and happily gave him the number.

I then phoned Paul and we had the most marvellous conversation. At last we could talk openly without the rest of the world listening. Speaking on the short-wave radio is far from private, as the frequencies are open for anyone to tune into and eavesdrop. Relieved that at last I had safely arrived, and delighted that my experiences had not put me off sailing, he promised to write me a long letter. We were both very reluctant to end the call, but as I was hoping Russel was going to contact me we said goodnight and I promised to phone him the next day. The one thing I really wanted was to feel Paul hug me. However, as we were not going to meet until September I knew that until then we would have to make do with telephone calls, radio contact and letters.

About five minutes later the barman said there was a call for me. Excitedly I picked up the receiver, expecting it to be my son.

'Where are you?' said the voice.

'La Coruna.'

'Whereabouts in Spain is that?'

Suddenly I realized with a shock that I was talking to my ex-husband, and that well-remembered, sickening feeling descended on me. He began to ask me all sorts of questions.

'Please can I talk to Russel?' was my only response.

'In a minute. First of all you can talk to me,' he insisted.

After a few moments, when I felt that he had no intention of letting me speak to Russel, I told him I would have to hang up as there were other people wanting to use the phone. I waited some time and then called again. This time, fortunately, Russel answered and we began to make plans for him to fly out, bringing my new sail and the other parts I needed to repair *Lucia*. We were both really excited that he was coming to see me. I arranged to speak to him again in a few days to confirm the date and time of his flight so that I could meet him at the airport with my ship's papers, just in case he had a problem bringing in so many strange items.

After the telephone calls, fatigue once again engulfed

me and I longed to return to *Lucia* and rest. The people I had met in the bar tried hard to persuade me to stay and join them in another drink, but I knew that if I accepted their hospitality I would be quite incapable of getting back aboard *Lucia*. Alcohol on top of exhaustion is not a good idea!

I said my goodbyes and, joined by Susan and David Evans, the British couple who had escorted me into the harbour, I made my way back to *Lucia*. They were very keen to come aboard and see what *Lucia* was like and, despite my tiredness, I invited them to do so. They seemed very impressed and, as they were leaving early the next morning, wanted to show me their yacht in return. How could I refuse? Exhausted or not, I accepted, and they took me in their dinghy to where they were moored. Luckily Susan soon saw how tired I was, and after a quick but appreciative tour of their boat I was returned to *Lucia*, all of us hoping we would meet again one day.

Once aboard *Lucia* I set about changing the bed linen – I really could not face putting my newly clean body into such smelly sheets. But when my head eventually hit the pillow the last thing my mind would allow me to do was sleep. All was peaceful and quiet; no wind screaming in the rigging, no rolling of the yacht, no flogging damaged headsail. There was nothing I needed to do – not even keep watch. But still I was unable to fall asleep. In the end I lay there and thought about the telephone conversations I had had that evening. All of them except one left me with a warm glow, and eventually I feel asleep.

I awoke with a start an hour later, not immediately aware of my surroundings. I started to rush up to see what was happening around me. As soon as I realised that I was safe in harbour, I sank back down in my bunk, laughing to myself. Sleeping for longer than one or two hours at a time was to evade me for about three weeks after my arrival in La Coruna. Little did I realise that this was to become a familiar pattern at the end of each of my passages.

The next morning as I sat in the cockpit, enthralled by the sights and sounds of this strange new place, I felt I wanted to venture forth and explore it. Unfortunately, however, my body was complaining bitterly about the unprecedented effort it had so recently endured. I did go ashore, but common sense told me my first port of call should be a masseur. I got money from a bank via my credit card and bought myself a comprehensive English–Spanish dictionary. Using the dictionary and sign language, I was able to communicate reasonably well and managed to find a beauty salon with a masseur.

Afterwards I felt wonderful, as if I was floating on air. Feeling very pleased with myself, I returned to the harbour for lunch in the marina bar, where I came across some of the people I had been introduced to in my exhausted state the night before. I was amazed at the speed with which friendships were formed between cruising folk. It seemed that, because yachts were swiftly moving from harbour to harbour, time was not wasted on the land-based principles of 'getting to know one another'. You were either accepted or not. So many of these like-minded people took me to their hearts, offering me advice and help on a multitude of subjects. I returned to *Lucia* awash with the milk of human kindness, where I rested and slept on and off for the remainder of the afternoon.

When I went on deck to watch the sunset I noticed a yacht that had moored opposite *Lucia*. Later that evening in the bar I met the guys on board, who had sailed from Ireland and by all accounts had had an eventful passage. Henry, the youngest member of the

Irish crew, entertained everyone with his theatrical re-
enactment of their voyage. We nicknamed him 'Henry
the Navigator'. It was not long before Geoff and a few
of the other people began telling their own stories, and
one of my newly acquired friends, Pat Dixon from
Tribute, began telling the assembled audience about my
own adventures. The skipper of the Irish yacht asked me
what my plans were. I explained that as soon as my son
arrived I was going to repair *Lucia*, and when all was
completed I would set sail once more for the Azores. He
gave me a very odd look, which at the time puzzled me.

As my body began to recover from the rigours of my
first solo passage I ventured further afield, enjoying the
wonders of my new surroundings. I did not waste a
minute of my time during the three weeks I waited for
Russel to arrive. When I was not off sightseeing, I was
either being entertained on other people's yachts or
returning the compliment on *Lucia*. I had suddenly found
myself amongst a warm and comfortable extended family.

On the morning of Russel's arrival I was working
hard to prepare *Lucia* before dashing off to meet him at
the airport when a knock on the hull interrupted my
labours. This was a familiar sound, announcing the
arrival of yet another visitor. I was fast running out of
time, and I popped my head out to explain as politely as
I could that I had no time to chat today. I was greeted
by a young man whom I had not met before. He asked
if he could speak to the skipper, and when I told him
that was me he at first looked a little surprised and then
asked if he could come aboard. I apologised again,
explaining my situation, but he was not put off.

'My name's Alan Bruce. I promise I won't take up
any of your time but I'd love to chat with you before
you leave. Also, I have a big favour I want to ask you.'

Before I could reply he was aboard and admiring
Lucia enthusiastically.

He explained that he was the skipper of a French catamaran moored in the harbour and had just sailed up from South Africa, encountering one disaster after another. He was unable to stop talking and, although with each new subject he promised he would give me the short version, it did not take me long to realise that that was a physical impossibility for Alan. The great favour he required was the loan of my socket set to help him repair his defunct engine. I agreed, issuing stern warnings about what I would do to him if he failed to return it safely to me.

Another knock on the hull. I groaned and asked Alan to send whoever it was away, as I really had no time to talk with anybody else. He looked out, then said:

'I'm afraid these are one group of people who you have no choice about talking to.'

I shot him a look of exasperation.

'It's the customs men,' he explained and promptly abandoned me, promising as he disappeared that he would return my tools that evening.

I had completely forgotten about the customs people, expecting a visit from them just after my arrival, not three weeks later. There were three of them, and thankfully they spoke a little English. Even so, they found it very hard to believe that I was the captain and sailing alone. After what seemed like an extremely long time they completed their paperwork and left. That was another new experience I had survived! I arrived at the airport only just in time to meet Russel. Fortunately he had no problems getting through customs himself with a huge sail bag bulging with all sorts of bits and pieces for *Lucia*. On the journey back we hardly stopped talking to draw breath as there was so much to catch up on. Russel had brought a huge bundle of post for me and, after he had gone to sleep that evening I eagerly opened my letters and read them until the early hours.

Paul had sent me a wonderful letter, enclosing clear instructions on how to remove *Lucia*'s unwanted furling system and fit a normal rigging screw to the front stay so that I could use a hank on sail. On paper this all looked straightforward, but in practice it was not long before Russel and I were pulling our hair out. However Alan was a great help, and I breathed a sigh of relief when eventually the job was completed. I went up and down my mast so often that some of the marina staff commented that I must enjoy it!

Although *Lucia* was well stocked with spares, there was no way I could carry every item I might need – and of course it's Murphy's law that you will have the right object but not quite the right size. I got to know the commercial area of La Coruna very well as I went in search of suppliers for the specialised parts I lacked. My dictionary was put to very good use. I found the patience of the traders I was dealing with exemplary, but soon discovered that the best way to obtain what I required was to take along a sample or a drawing. Sometimes I was unable to buy exactly what I wanted. Then I would call on my new-found friends to see if they could assist me. The exchange trade between cruising folk is legendary, and it was not long before I had everything I needed.

Russel spent five very busy days with me. When we were not working on *Lucia* we were partying. Alan and Russel got on extremely well and spent the evenings encouraging one another to consume vast quantities of alcohol. All too soon it was time for Russel to return to England; when we set off for the airport he was, unsurprisingly, suffering from a dreadful hangover. After his plane had taken off I felt very sad, as I had no idea when I would see him again.

Back at the harbour Alan was there to keep me company and we chatted for hours. He told me some amazing things about Russel.

'He's asked me to look after you while you're here.'

'Oh, isn't that sweet of him?' I replied.

'Yes. He's really quite worried about you – feels you're very naïve when it comes to men and asked me to make sure you were not taken advantage of.'

To say I was shocked is an understatement, especially when Alan assured me that he intended to keep his promise because he agreed with Russel's sentiments. While all three of us had been together I had felt like a mother not only to Russel but also to Alan. This was a most unexpected role reversal!

Alan was true to his word and, although I went out on the town with all the other yachties, he stuck to me like glue. We spent many hours talking; I listened enthusiastically as he told me about his forthcoming marriage, while he listened sympathetically to my past history and with eagerness to my plans for *Lucia*. One day he gave me a book called *Bridge Across My Sorrows*, the harrowing true-life story of an Irish woman, Christina Noble. Inside he had written this inscription:

To a rising star,

People who dream at night wake in the morning to find their dreams have faded. People who dream by day are dangerous people because they fulfil their dreams.

I know you will fulfil yours!

He told me that until meeting me this woman had been his number one hero, but now I had taken her place. I felt honoured.

CHAPTER EIGHT

LA CORUNA TOWARDS FAIAL

While waiting patiently in La Coruna for a good weather forecast I restocked *Lucia* with food, water and fuel. By 26 June fog had arrived, lasting from early morning until late afternoon. After the second day of these conditions I began to think I would never set sail. But people with local knowledge assured me that once clear of the harbour the mist would disappear. With Alan's help I moved *Lucia* out of the marina on to a mooring buoy to await my departure. On the morning of the 29th I decided to put my nose out and give it a try. At 1000 hours I slipped my mooring lines, waved fond farewells to the many friends I had made, and motored out of the harbour. We were bound once more for the island of Faial in the Azores.

Motor sailing with just the jib unfurled, trying to catch a wind that hardly existed, we continued to put distance between the harbour and ourselves. Contrary to my information, the mist did not clear. However, I decided not to return to the harbour as in such conditions I felt safer the further we were from land. I was glad I had put on my thermal underwear as there was a penetrating chill in the air.

That first night at sea was very worrying indeed. Fog and mist are not my favourite weather conditions on land, but at sea they take on a whole new meaning. By now, as there was just a hint of a breeze, I had raised the main sail and we continued to motor sail at approximately four knots. As night fell I slowed *Lucia* down a little. It was difficult to ascertain how far I could see, and as I knew there would be other shipping about I proceeded cautiously, not daring to close my eyes even for a minute.

Joshua, my wind vane self-steering, was having great difficulty staying on course in such light winds. Also Charlie, the electronic autopilot, had stopped working and I had to stay at the helm for many hours to keep *Lucia* on course. Eventually – I have no idea why – Charlie decided to work after a fashion. Thankfully this gave me a little respite and I managed to close my eyes for a few minutes between keeping watch.

The conditions were eerie. As I looked up to the top of my mast to check that my strobe light was working it appeared as if the mast had poked a hole in the fog. I could just make out a few stars, but at sea level the mist was still very dense.

At midnight, while sitting in the cockpit plotting my position on the chart, I confirmed that we were deep in the shipping lane. Anxiously I kept casting my eyes to the top of the mast to check on my navigation lights, hoping that if any ships had failed to spot me on their radar they would be able to see me by eye.

Suddenly I heard a sound from behind and my skeleton almost jumped out of my skin. There, very close to my stern, was a massive ship. It looked like Harrods on Christmas Eve, aglow with white lights, and it was moving very fast behind me. I quickly looked all around – the mist had lifted a little and I could just make out the lights of other vessels coming at *Lucia* from what looked like every angle. I immediately took the helm, but only changed course for one ship that I felt was a bit too close for comfort. I was probably being over-cautious, but one near miss was enough for me!

After that incident, staying awake became less of a problem. Although trying to stare through the fog to see what was ahead and all around was exhausting, my imagination was far too active to allow me to sleep. When dawn eventually broke it revealed an overcast sky and a thick mist at sea level. Thankfully, by 0800 hours the mist began to clear.

Suddenly the sea was alive with dolphins; it was pure joy to see them after such a traumatic night. Very soon the sun appeared and it became an absolutely beautiful day. The sea was milky calm, but of course there was not a breath of wind. I went forward to set the light weather genoa and was delighted when one of the dolphins shot out in front of *Lucia*'s bows. I watched, mesmerised, as this beautiful black and white creature gambolled about very close to her, apparently for no other reason than to give me pleasure. I went below to fetch my camera and took endless photos of him to remind me of this wonderful moment.

It took me quite a long time to set the sail as before leaving harbour I had tied it very securely to the port side guardrail, and of course the wind direction dictated that it be set on the starboard side. By the time I had rearranged and raised the sail I had worked up quite a sweat. I went below, stripped down to my underwear and then sat in the cockpit, bathing my body in the light breeze and warm sunshine.

As I sat there relaxing I recalled the long talk I had had with Paul on the radio that morning, during which he told me that my dear friend Philip Rose had left Bideford in *Kittiwake* with a young Frenchman aboard as crew. They too were bound for the harbour of Horta in Faial. I daydreamed about the wonderful party Philip and I would have when we met in Horta.

I had a great time for the rest of that day. First I treated myself to a cockpit bath, which consisted of one bowl of warm water and a jug to sluice myself down with. Feeling totally refreshed I went below and cooked myself a meal, which I took up to the bows so that I could gaze at the vast empty ocean surrounding us as I ate it. Just as the sun was setting I opened a present that my friend Anne Hammick had given me before I left Falmouth. We had planned to meet in Horta, where Anne was flying in her role as press officer for the Azab race, a sailing event from Falmouth to the Azores and back. Unfortunately, due to my diversion to La Coruna, I would be arriving too late to keep our rendezvous. Back in Falmouth, when Anne handed me the present, she told me that I must not open it until I was south of 44 degrees. I remembered her laughing at my incomprehension. Inside was a wonderful assortment of goodies, including a miniature bottle of Martini and tonic. The enclosed card read: 'Congratulations, Mo, on reaching the halfway mark.' Anne must have thought I was really stupid not to have realised the significance of her instructions. I drank a toast thanking her for such a great present and asking the powers that be to help me make it safely into my desired harbour this time.

That night I was able to rest much more easily, getting a good twenty minutes' sleep between keeping watch. It was just as well, for the next day the winds were very light and when I started the engine it emitted a loud squealing noise. Since I am not in the least way mechanically inclined, this noise concerned me a great deal. It was quite likely that anxiety about the engine

Right: *Lucia* under construction, July 1992. Sheets of steel were welded on to her frames and stringers to form the hull.

Left: *Lucia*'s completed interior showing the main cabin. In the foreground is the galley; tucked in on the right is the chart table; and in the centre of the picture you can see the door which leads into the fore-cabin.

Right: Launch day, 20 February 1994! You can just see the bottle of champagne which Philip eventually managed to break over *Lucia*'s bows.

Above: Stepping *Lucia*'s forty-five-foot mast, June 1994, which finally transformed her into a beautiful ocean sailing yacht.

Left: My first single-handed voyage. *Lucia* and I sailed from Falmouth Marina on 19 May 1995. Philip, Russel, Stuart, Sheila and Paul [below] gathered to watch me sail out to sea.

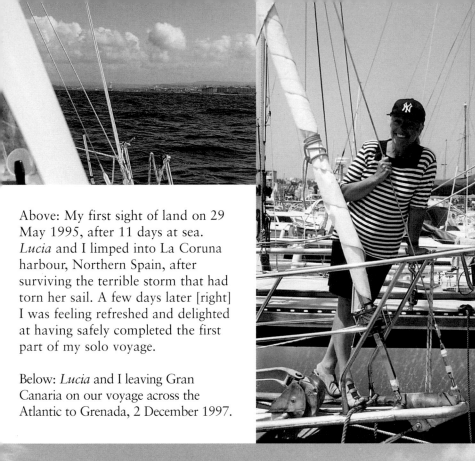

Above: My first sight of land on 29 May 1995, after 11 days at sea. *Lucia* and I limped into La Coruna harbour, Northern Spain, after surviving the terrible storm that had torn her sail. A few days later [right] I was feeling refreshed and delighted at having safely completed the first part of my solo voyage.

Below: *Lucia* and I leaving Gran Canaria on our voyage across the Atlantic to Grenada, 2 December 1997.

Above: *Lucia* (on the right) taking part in the celebration sail past in Newport, Rhode Island, 27 June 1998.

Above: Me in *Lucia*'s bows letting Neptune 'kiss' my toes!

Above: *Lucia* in all her glory proudly sailing the ocean waves

was what brought on my first feeling of nausea on this trip. I eventually narrowed the problem down to the fan belt or the alternator. When I outlined the symptoms to Paul over the radio, he confirmed my diagnosis. What is more, he was confident that if necessary I could rectify the problem.

Fortunately, I had a reprieve: the wind strength increased, so I was able to turn off the engine. I went forward to lower the light weather sail in order to raise the working jib. I used a great deal of energy while stuffing it back into its bag, and before long I was offering the contents of my stomach to the fish over the bows. I remember cheerfully thinking that it made a change from throwing up over the stern.

By dawn next day the wind had become very light once more and I started the engine, hoping that the previous day's problem would have disappeared. But within a few minutes the squealing noise became unbearable and the alternator was no longer charging the batteries. I stopped the engine and collected up the tools I thought I would need. The engine is housed beneath the companionway steps, which I had to remove before lowering the cover to gain access. On inspection, I discovered that the alternator bracket had broken. Thankfully, Paul had provided me with two spare brackets in anticipation of this problem. But what would have taken a mechanic approximately thirty minutes to fix took me almost five hours. I had to keep stopping what I was doing because of acute seasickness, and all too soon was feeling very sorry for myself.

The last part of the job was to tighten the fan belt connecting the alternator to the front pulley of the engine. To begin with I used my crowbar as a lever, pushing down with one foot as I bent to tighten the nuts. But as I balanced like this in the rolling, pitching yacht, my foot kept slipping on the metal. I replaced the crowbar with my broom handle, which, being a longer lever, made it possible for me to sit on it while I tightened the nuts. I had to be very careful, as I was sure the wooden handle would break under such pressure and an accident was the last thing I needed. Then my stomach called a halt to the job in hand once more. As I held my head over the sink, heaving, with nothing but bile left to bring up, my head began to throb unbearably. It took me a little time to recover enough strength to continue with the task, and when I carefully sat on the broom handle again the prime thought in my mind was: slowly does it, but for goodness sake get this damn job done. The very moment I completed the task the handle broke, but I was well prepared for it and thankfully received no injuries – just a quickening of my heart rate.

By now the wind had died completely and, with no engine to control her movement either, *Lucia* had begun to wallow in the swell, which was not helping my delicate stomach one bit. I started the engine and held my breath: it ran beautifully and started charging the batteries immediately, to my extreme relief. We motor sailed for the next four hours until the wind returned, during which time I sat in the cockpit relaxing. Eventually the seasickness began to fade.

During the late afternoon I spotted a merchant ship approaching me on my starboard side. As we were sailing by then and I did not want to alter course I called them up on the VHF radio to make sure they had seen me. The radio officer of the German vessel *Pasewalk* assured me they had spotted me on their radar some time ago and were just about to change course, which they immediately did. We chatted for a short time, asking each other where we were bound and so on. Then he asked me how many crew were aboard. 'Just me,' I responded.

The ship then changed course again and passed very

close astern of *Lucia*. I was delighted to see the crew lining the decks, cheering and waving at me with great vigour, while the ship's horn sounded a dozen times or more. I found this a very moving experience and a great boost to my morale. I hoped the crew were unaware that I was wearing only my thermal vest and long-johns!

When I talked to Paul that evening he was delighted that I had cured the mechanical problem and assured me that it mattered not a jot how long I took. He passed on messages from my sister and Russel, which added to my feeling of contentment. As I settled into my nightly routine of keeping watch, I concluded that all in all it hadn't been such a bad day!

Over the next few days, considering the wind was light and variable I made reasonably good progress, fluctuating between sailing and motor sailing. I was by now in daily contact with an American couple, who were passing me information they had received from their on-board weather fax. Len and Kitty were sailing to Rhode Island, USA, from the Azores on their fifty-two-foot aluminium yacht *Dulcimer*. Apart from being very informative, I found these daily chats most enjoyable. Len and Kitty gave me their home telephone number and offered me the use of their mooring in North Carolina if ever I should find myself in that part of the world.

But Len was also the bearer of bad news. He told me that David Sinnett-Jones, who had set sail from Wales in his Spray *Zane Spray*, bound for the centenary celebrations in Horta, was having serious problems. His yacht appeared to have sprung a leak and David had been forced to turn back when he was 200 miles from land. Len promised to keep me informed of further developments. I tried to put my concern for David to one side and concentrate on getting as much rest as possible while I had the chance. By now I was managing to eat very light meals and, thankfully, keeping it where it belonged. If this continued I would soon be full of energy.

I felt well enough to start the book Paul had given me, Joshua Slocum's *Sailing Alone Around the World*, which was so well written that I found it a joy to read. When I read Joshua's account of his first single-handed trip approximately twenty-five miles along the coast of Massachusetts, from Boston to Gloucester Harbor, I was delighted to find that he had experienced similar emotions to me. As he rounded the outer pier at East Boston, 'A thrilling pulse beat high within me.' Then as he entered Gloucester harbour alone he exclaims that he does so 'With my heart in my mouth'. Joshua undertook this trip, as he put it, 'To weigh the voyage and my feelings and all that'. I was surprised to discover that, after he had completed preparations in Gloucester for his round-the-world voyage, he too embarked in May. What a coincidence that, quite unwittingly, I should have set sail a hundred years and just a few days later.

This aroused my curiosity and I wondered what, as an experienced sea captain, he would have thought of this crazy woman, a complete novice, trying to cross half an ocean on her own. Well, no matter what he would have thought I was going to keep on trying. Who knows, maybe one day I would feel I had achieved a little of what he had accomplished. Then, feeling queasy again, I put the book down, hoping that it would not be too long before I could read a little more.

I scanned the horizon each day in the hope of spying a sail that would turn out to be Philip's yacht *Kittiwake*. I also spent many hours sitting on the bows of *Lucia*, studying my environment, and was rewarded by some amazing sights of marine life. The first time I saw flying fish I was filled with wonder. They leaped from the sea and flew for great distances, looking for all the world like a flock of small birds, until they suddenly disappeared beneath the waves. I always hoped they had escaped from the predator that was chasing them. Such experiences filled me with awe, and sometimes I would gaze in the direction of the Azores and wonder how such small islands could survive in such a vast ocean.

There had been very little wind for days now and, although before embarking on my voyage I imagined that being becalmed would be a peaceful experience, in practice it was anything but. The swell of the ocean would roll *Lucia*, spilling any wind from her sails, and the noise of the rig banging around became very annoying. I expended a great deal of energy trying to sail *Lucia* only to give up, drop the sails and start the engine. Then at the hint of a breeze I would raise them again and motor sail for a while, only to have to repeat the exhausting procedure.

Maybe it was because I was feeling very tired and frustrated with these conditions that my mind kept wandering to the past. After finding these thoughts catching me unawares, I decided to confront them and put my feelings down on my tape recorder. This took a great deal of courage, as a big part of me wanted to do as I had always done and push these memories as far away as possible. However, the sea is a great leveller. If I could not be honest with myself alone on the ocean, where could I? I sat down in the cockpit, took some very deep breaths and allowed my innermost feelings to rise to the surface. I gazed at the sea as I poured my heartfelt thoughts into the unbiased, unemotional machine. Once my emotional dam was breached, there was no stopping it: silent tears ran down my face as I recorded my long hidden memories.

One question I kept asking myself: why had I endured my unhappy marriage for so long? Why had I tolerated my husband's behaviour? As I allowed myself to remember way back to my first love, suddenly the answer appeared to me as clear as the beautiful blue sky!

I was just fourteen when I met Stewart; we attended the same school. After a few months our relationship became very involved and my parents were shocked at the intensity of our love. However, to Stewart and me it seemed the most natural thing in the world. We had no doubts that we would spend the rest of our lives together. Three years later, when Stewart was eighteen, he was killed in a motorbike accident. I was totally devastated and found life without him unbearable. I withdrew into myself and began talking to him constantly in my mind, pleading with him to come and fetch me as I lacked the courage to commit suicide. When this failed, I begged him to find a way of returning to me.

Some time later, while I was walking along the road with my younger sister Sheila, I saw Stewart walking towards me. The three of us started talking, though Stewart acted as if we were strangers. He arranged to meet us later that evening at the local fair and then casually walked away. I watched him in complete silence as he turned around to wave and smile at us. My sister commented on the fact that the young man was the living image of Stewart. To me, however, my prayers had been answered. My dead lover had at last returned. The three of us met later at the fair and I continued to feel my dreams had come true. We arranged to go on our first proper date the following evening.

The next night when this young man came to collect me from my parents' home my mother almost shut the door on him because she was so astounded at his incredible likeness to Stewart. She pleaded with me not to go out with him, as she was afraid for me. That night during our date we spent most of the time in each other's arms and I had no idea what the film we had gone to see was about. Afterwards we went into London from the distant suburb where my parents lived, and for hours I watched and listened to this young man intently. Although there were a lot of aspects of his personality that were unlike Stewart's, I made excuses for them to make them fit.

It was the early hours of the morning before I returned to my parents' house. Even then, I did not want to part from him. I remember saying that I felt I had known him all my life, but confessed that I could not remember his name!

This threw the young man. 'You mean you've been snogging with me all night and you can't remember my name?'

'I'm really sorry. I don't mean to upset you, but that's exactly what I mean.'

He then reminded me of his name and asked me to meet him again the following evening. I remembered feeling strange when his name was not Stewart, but once more I invented some excuse to cover this unacceptable fact.

Over the next few months, although I held back at first, I eventually allowed him to make love to me. I knew deep down it was wrong, but I was desperate to feel physically bound to Stewart again. If I had been less obsessed with Stewart's memory I would have finished the relationship at that point. Very soon I discovered I was pregnant.

It was only when I reluctantly agreed to marry this young man that I stopped having illusions about his identity. As I met him outside the registry office before the ceremony I at last summoned up the courage to tell him that if he did not want to go ahead it was all right. We could just walk away, and later we could explain to our guests that we had had a change of heart. He looked at me as if I was crazy and told me that of course he had not changed his mind. With a very heavy heart, I went through with the marriage. The one thought continually running through my mind was the prospect of divorce.

I now realised that I had stayed in my marriage because I had felt so bad about allowing myself to go through with it. I had decided to take complete responsibility for this person's happiness because of my guilty secret. I accepted the way he treated me only because I had been the one to make the mistake of marrying him. I am sure that deep down my husband knew I had never loved him, and that is why I always felt he treated me as an object he was trying to possess. I now chose to do my best to forgive him for any wrong he had done to me. I accepted that he was probably unable to help himself, and that it was I who was really at fault for not having had the courage to finish our relationship before the fateful marriage took place.

When the machine clicked off as it came to the end of the tape, I sat there completely drained. After a very long pause, I rewound the tape. Then, with my finger hovering over the play button, I realised that to hear my words was going to be very painful. However, I felt compelled to depress the button. But as the tape whirled forward, there was complete silence; I stared at the machine in disbelief. I repeatedly ran the tape forward and pressed 'Play', but still there was nothing. I reached the end of tape; there was not a single word on it!

The sense of relief was wonderful, though how this strange error had occurred I will never know. I began to laugh as I realised that somehow I had been given the opportunity to express my innermost thoughts without having to endure the pain of ever listening to them again. A wonderful feeling of peace descended on me as the enormity of my revelations dawned on me. One thought that kept leaping to the forefront of my mind was that I need no longer carry the guilt I had felt for years. I had always known deep in my heart that throughout my marriage I had done my best to be a good wife. My ex-husband's shock when he heard that I wanted to end what he considered an excellent marriage only confirmed that belief. Now I felt totally justified in forgiving myself for any wrong that I had committed by trying to replace Stewart with him, solely because he looked so like my dead lover. At last I could lay my past to rest and live the remainder of my life in the light of this knowledge. I also had the added comfort that, if ever the need arose again, I could voice my thoughts aloud to the wind and let it carry them away, leaving my soul refreshed.

CHAPTER NINE

FAIAL: A TOUGH GOAL TO REACH

By 5 July I was very concerned about fuel, as I had some 500 miles to cover before arriving at the island of Faial. I went below and carefully made my way under the cockpit to look at the fuel sight tube on the outside of the tank. On a moving boat it is not easy to get an accurate reading, but I judged that I had twenty-five gallons left in the tank. I also had two five-gallon containers, which I dragged from under the cockpit and lifted on to *Lucia*'s stern. With the aid of a funnel I carefully poured them into the tank, doing my best not to spill a single drop of this precious liquid.

I recalculated that I only had enough fuel to continue in my present, motor sailing mode for 350 miles. Without an increase in the wind I would not make Faial. I studied the chart for some time and found that the island of Sao Miguel was the nearest piece of land to my present position, at just over 300 miles away. There was nothing else for it: I tacked and set a course for this other island in the Azores group, hoping that my calculations were correct.

I was determined not to let this change of plan dampen my spirits. After all, at least this time I would be a great deal closer to my desired destination. I also had other things to occupy my mind: there was a white light showing on the engine panel, which indicated that I had got another problem with the alternator. On checking the batteries, I was relieved to see that they were still being charged. There were no strange noises coming from the engine, and when I looked at the panel again I saw that the light had gone out. I had no idea what to make of this. It would have been great to dismiss it from my mind, but that was not possible. I would just have to monitor the situation and hope that if push came to shove I would be able to repair the damn thing once more.

As the day progressed the sun came out and it turned into an almost perfect day. Suddenly I became very hungry and decided to cook myself a huge meal. It all had to be out of tins, unfortunately, but I made up for this by laying the cockpit table properly and dishing the food up on to a china plate. No eating out of the pan this time! With a flat, calm sea and a tablecloth made of non-slip material I had the confidence to go the whole hog and drink from a glass. It was only water, but given the mood I was in it could easily have been the finest white wine. Feeling very happy, I sat in the sunshine and enjoyed what to me seemed like a banquet.

A little later I got my sextant out for the first time and took three sights at approximately five-minute intervals. The angles were all quite close together, which would indicate that I had shot the sights correctly. However, when I calculated one of them and compared it to my GPS reading I was almost two degrees out. This might not seem much to non-sailors, but it was approximately 120 nautical miles. I concluded that I must have done something wrong. As I studied the sight reduction tables, I began to feel a little queasy. Not wishing to give the fish the benefit of my wonderful meal, I decided I would postpone the astro navigation until the next day.

The rest of the day passed blissfully, and as I watched the setting sun a feeling of excitement began to rise deep within me. Maybe tonight the clear sky would hold and I would be able to watch the stars and planets appear. It did, and I could. There was almost a full moon, and when it was at its zenith the reflection on the ocean was pure magic. A large shoal of fish had surrounded me for many days, and that night as they jostled for position their silver bellies gave them the appearance of moon-beams. Staying in the cockpit for most of the night as I did not want to miss a moment of this wonderful spectacle, I felt as if I was in Never Never Land.

Yet again the next morning, due to poor radio conditions I was unable to talk directly with Paul; however, we did manage to pass messages to each other via the UK Maritime Net. He approved of my change of plan and looked forward to talking with me over the phone as soon as I got into harbour. In the meantime, we agreed to keep trying to make radio contact just in case conditions improved and we got lucky.

Each day at 0800 hours, I would listen into the UK Maritime Net. The frequency is manned by a wonderful group of volunteer radio hams. Yachts sailing in many different parts of the world check in, giving their positions and any useful information about the conditions they are experiencing. The net does its best to provide up-to-date weather forecasts and is a great source of help and encouragement to yachts in transit, not least *Lucia*. I made friends with many of the operators and will always be grateful for their help in relaying messages and supplying information.

When I tuned into the agreed frequency at 1300 hours

that day to talk to Len on *Dulcimer*, he told me that for
several days now he had been trying his hand at fishing
but so far had had no luck. I told him about my
devoted escort and he became really excited.

'How many have you managed to hook?'

'None, Len. I couldn't possibly bring myself to kill
and eat any of them.'

'Then hook them in and eat them alive!'

I giggled over this suggestion, while I wished him luck
with his own efforts.

As Len related the latest news regarding David
Sinnett-Jones and his girlfriend Susan, my heart went
out to them. The coastguard had been alerted to their
predicament, as David and Susan were now continually
manning the pumps. Len and I felt it would only be a
matter of time before something would have to be done
to assist them.

After my radio schedule, I continued without success
to try and sail *Lucia*. We were now in a high-pressure
area, which resulted in whatever wind there was dying
completely by late afternoon. I was compelled to revert
once more to motor sailing. But today, just ten minutes
after starting the engine the warning light glared at me
once more. This time when I checked the ammeter I saw
that the batteries were only being trickle-charged, so I
knew it was essential to examine the engine. I was
extremely relieved to see that the bracket I had replaced
on the alternator was still intact. Thankfully, this time
the problem appeared to be nothing more than a slack
fan belt. I did my best to tighten the belt, and hoped it
would remain taut until I reached harbour.

Totally without warning, at 2000 hours the wind
piped up and we began to race along. I stopped the
engine, rushed forward and dropped the light weather
genoa before it could split. Then I raised the working
jib. With the wind in its present direction, I needed to

sail downwind to maintain my desired course. This involved refurling the jib, setting up the spinnaker pole, connecting it to the sail and then unfurling the jib again. As this was an unfamiliar manoeuvre to me, I decided instead to sail a little off course until I was sure the wind would continue from its present direction.

I was glad I had showed restraint, as the wind died very quickly and we had to revert to motor sailing yet again. My worry about fuel made it impossible for me to relax though, and as soon as I felt a slight breeze I switched the engine off and reset the sails. The result was a night of very little rest as the rig banged and crashed around in the very light wind. At one point I felt a complete failure as a sailor; no matter what I did to the sheets, I simply could not set the sails correctly. Then I realised that the wind had changed direction again. This time I altered course slightly to make the best of what was on offer. I went below to rest, but suffered hours and hours of rolling around. Due to the light winds, the speed we were making was not enough to propel *Lucia* forward through the steep swell.

At 0400 hours the wind materialised from yet another direction. I reset the sails and we began to romp along. It felt really wonderful; once more I started to enjoy life, as I was finding it possible to rest reasonably well – so much, in fact, that I almost missed my early morning sked with Paul. This time conditions were great and we were able to have a long chat and catch up on all our news. At last he was able to pass on the many messages he had received from my family and friends.

Later in the day, I saw the first ship I had seen since my pleasant encounter with the German vessel *Pasewalk*. When I first spotted it, I thought it was a sail on the horizon. I rushed to get my binoculars, thinking it might just be Philip in *Kittiwake*, but it was the bridge of a ship showing white against the sky. I called them on the

VHF radio but received no response; they just continued on their course and motored past *Lucia* about a mile away.

During my usual sked with Len, he told me the dreadful news that *Zane Spray* had sunk some two hundred miles south-west of Ireland. But David and Susan had been rescued and were now on dry land. Rudi, a radio ham speaking from Falmouth, was also on frequency, and between the two of them they did their best to cheer me up. When I complained about my lack of prolonged wind, they decided to whistle it up for me – until, between my giggles, I begged them to stop. I questioned the wisdom of their act, as whistling at sea is traditionally considered to bring sailors bad luck. But Len assured me I had nothing to worry about, as their efforts could hardly be described as real whistling. I had to agree – even my kettle could have given a better musical rendition.

Having suffered another day of light, variable winds, by nightfall I was feeling pretty ragged. I would love to have gone below to rest, but having seen more vessels on the horizon I decided to stay in the cockpit until dawn. At 0300 hours I was just thinking that Len and Rudi's efforts had not proved effective when the wind miraculously increased and *Lucia* was able to sail. By the time I snuggled down into my bunk, I was cold and very tired. The wind was still steadily blowing, so all was peaceful and I was able to sleep soundly until my sked with Paul.

Today he gave me the very disappointing news that Philip had been forced to turn back five days into his voyage. Unfortunately, his crew member had been struck down badly with seasickness. Philip had tried many things, including spoon-feeding him honey. But when he failed to respond Philip knew he could rapidly weaken and might even die, so he returned to Falmouth. I worried how, at Philip's time of life, he would take this blow, and learned later that he felt so devastated he had decided to sell his boat.

Was it the knowledge of Philip's aborted trip, or the fact that the wind had died yet again, leaving us wallowing in a very steep sea? Whichever, I recorded in my log that my normal buoyant mood had taken a tumble and I felt very low. It was now 8 July and I had hoped to make landfall by the 9th, but due to my slow progress this looked unlikely. I did my best to boost my morale by assuring myself that I would eventually get there, and that was the most important thing.

That night the beautiful sky began to soothe my troubled mind. With a full moon it was almost like daylight, and once more I spent the night keeping watch in the cockpit. By dawn I was feeling ravenous and cooked an enormous breakfast of eggs, mushrooms and beans. I amazed myself by eating every morsel. I then fell into a deep sleep, and without the aid of my alarm I would never have managed to keep watch.

When I was fully awake I plotted my position on the chart and realised we were making dreadfully slow progress. I spent an hour fiddling around trying to find the best point of sail. The wind was now coming from the west, the direction in which I wanted to head, so that was impossible. In addition, the current was stronger than I had anticipated and we were being pushed in an easterly direction. It was time to make big decisions. I spread out the chart and studied the effects of heading in this or that direction. In the end, I set *Lucia* on a course of 310 degrees, proposing to cover thirty-five miles; then I planned to tack and head in a south-westerly direction. I hoped that this would put me fairly close to Sao Miguel by mid-afternoon the next day.

Having settled on a positive course of action, I felt a

great deal better. Knowing that, God willing, I would soon be in harbour, I decided it was time to blitz the galley. It looked as if World War III had been in full swing down below. Two hours later I stood back happily to admire my handiwork. Then it was my turn. I would love to have washed my hair, but *Lucia*'s motion would not have made this an easy activity. Even an all-over wash was a tricky manoeuvre. By the time I had struggled into some clean clothes I felt I had accomplished quite a lot for one day. Feeling very pleased with myself, I took my RDF into the cockpit and managed to pick up the radio beacon on the island very quickly. It was such a comfort to get confirmation that the island was where I thought it should be, even if I could not see it.

I was so pleased I had tackled my domestic chores early in the day, because before long the seas began to build and *Lucia*'s progress was being thwarted in an extremely uncomfortable way. We were really struggling to make headway, and by 1400 hours I was beginning to despair. The wind was right on the nose and the seas were unbelievably steep. I continued to try every trick I had learnt and a few more besides, but to no avail. As *Lucia* pounded into the waves, every third one would bring her to a shuddering stop.

A strange noise from behind stopped me in my tracks. At first I thought it must be the sound of the waves, and then I saw a very large, black shadow beneath the surface of the water. I thought I must be seeing things – surely it could not be a whale! I watched spellbound as this huge creature surfaced about thirty feet away on my starboard side and blew gently. I still thought he was a figment of my imagination. I should have been terrified, but at that moment I felt only wonder and excitement. He was very inquisitive and began to circle *Lucia*. Then he dived beneath the waves and resurfaced about ten feet from my stern. I was now able to assess his size as about twenty feet long. I would love to have gone below for my camera, but did not dare take my eyes off him for a second.

A thought crossed my mind: because of his size he was probably quite young, and maybe his mother was close at hand. If so, would she consider *Lucia* a threat? My excitement switched to worry as I watched him circle *Lucia*, closer and closer. He became very playful, diving under her bow as if she were a toy. As *Lucia* was being tossed around in these huge seas, I became really worried that he would crash into us, damaging himself and putting a big dent in *Lucia*'s hull. For about ten minutes I felt sick with fear. At one point he was within five feet of us and I thought this was just too close for comfort. How much longer could he avoid a collision?

I waited until he was a little further away and then started the engine, in the hope that this would encourage him to keep his distance. However, it did not deter him one bit and he continued to play, circling very close. When he dived under *Lucia* amidships I quickly stopped the engine and held my breath. What did he plan to do next? Luckily, he just continued to enjoy himself without inflicting damage on either of us. After he had spent about three-quarters of an hour with me, he disappeared into the deep. As I sat pondering this incredible encounter, my emotions switched from frustration at my lack of progressive sailing, to sheer gratitude at having been given the chance to experience this amazing event.

Before nightfall I plotted my position on the chart and found we were only thirty miles south of the island. As I scanned the horizon I felt disappointed that all I could see was dark gathering clouds instead of the longed for land. Conditions began to deteriorate, so I deep reefed the mainsail, set the storm jib and did my best to sail in the direction I wanted – but without success. By now I was feeling very seasick, either through the combination of excitement and fear at having seen the whale, or else because of *Lucia*'s very uncomfortable motion.

That evening I tried to make contact with Paul as arranged, but could only manage to relay my position to him. I took my sleeping bag into the cockpit and was able to sleep for a short time, but awoke with a dreadful headache. When I tried to swallow some painkillers they immediately made me very sick. Feeling too exhausted to be of any use to *Lucia*, I curled up in my sleeping bag and thankfully fell asleep once more. At 0400 hours I plotted my position on the chart, only to discover that we were being pushed further and further from the island. My spirits sank to a very low ebb.

Feeling totally powerless, I sought the comfort of my warm sleeping bag again. But strange noises interrupted my fitful rest. As I peered anxiously into the darkness, I wondered if my whale had returned along with his family. After a while, when I had been unable to see anything, I told myself not to let my imagination torment me.

The next time I awoke, I was astounded to see it was daylight. I must have been really exhausted to have slept so soundly, and I certainly felt much better. There on the horizon, directly in line with *Lucia*'s bow, was land. Excitement overwhelmed me – to make landfall after thirteen days is a very special thing. I plotted my position to confirm it was Sao Miguel, and was not at all surprised to find that we had lost five miles over the ground during the night. We were now thirty-five miles south-east of the island. I went forward to the mast to enjoy the view and became very emotional as I sang my own words in a not very tuneful version of Rod Stewart's 'Sailing': 'We are sailing, *Lucia* and I, across this vast, vast ocean. We have landfall; we have landfall. Oh, how fortunate we are . . . .'

When I had recovered my composure, I got to work on *Lucia* with renewed energy. I shook out the reef in the mainsail, put the storm jib away and unfurled the working jib. I then set her on the best possible course towards the island. I still felt a bit queasy, this time probably due to my stomach being so empty. I forced myself to nibble on some digestive biscuits while I waited for the appointed hour to call Paul. Conditions were not brilliant, but I was able to give him my position and tell him that I could see land. He sounded almost as excited as me and told me he was longing to speak to me on the phone.

I then tuned into the Maritime Net to give the operator my position and the good news of sighting land. Bill, the net operator that day, told me that another sailing vessel called *Kite* had been trying to raise me on the VHF. They too were heading for Sao Miguel, and from their position were not too far away. I tried to call *Kite*, but received no response. When I went back on deck I searched all around for them through my binoculars, but drew a blank.

By now the wind had become very light and I was constantly adjusting the sails to gain as much speed as possible. I continued to sail until our speed dropped below three knots and then I started the engine, praying that I would not run out of fuel before we had made it into harbour.

To conserve our supplies, I gently motor sailed at no more than four knots. I studied the pilot book to familiarise myself with the landmarks of the harbour entrance, and then keyed a waypoint into the GPS. The harbour of Ponta Delgada is situated at the south-west end of the island and I was concerned to see that we still had several miles to cover. Getting there before nightfall would be touch and go. I read the pilot book again, this time looking for suitable spots to drop anchor should it become necessary. Having made contingency plans, I felt able to relax for a while.

As I got closer to the island I was overwhelmed at its lush, green beauty, with small villages rising from the shore into the hills. My excitement was rising by the moment as I contemplated exploring this new land. A voice crackling over my VHF radio stopped my day-dreaming. I listened hard to try and make out the words, but it was impossible. A few minutes later I clearly heard the word '*Lucia*', and I responded immediately.

'Vessel calling *Lucia*, please go to channel seven.'

I called again when I had switched channels, but I could barely hear a voice and not the words spoken.

'Vessel calling *Lucia*, I'm returning to channel sixteen. Please try and call again later.'

I took up my binoculars and could just make out a small, dark shape far behind me. I wondered if it was *Kite*, the yacht that had apparently been trying to make contact with me. One hour later I gave them a call.

'*Kite*, *Kite*, this is *Lucia*. Over.'

'*Lucia* . . . crackle-crackle-crackle . . . *Kite*.'

I asked them to switch channels once more. This time, although their transmission was very broken, I was able to confirm that they were the dot just visible behind me.

They told me their sails were dark tan in colour and their hull was red. After a while we were able to exchange names. Mark and Polly were pretty sure they would not make harbour before dark and planned to go in at first light the next day. We had to cut our conversation short as they were having problems with their radio, but agreed to meet once we were all in harbour.

As the afternoon slipped by, I prepared *Lucia* for harbour. I was feeling very tired, and so to keep my concentration up I started singing, 'Ten green bottles hanging on the wall'. When I got fed up with that I went on to 'This man went to mow,' changing the words to 'This Mo went to sea'.

At 2100 hours I could see the port hand light of the

harbour entrance. It was so tempting – did I dare go in with the failing light, or should I turn round and find a spot to drop anchor until daylight? From the pilot book the harbour entrance looked straightforward. I decided to go for it, promising myself that if, when I got closer, I was not happy, I would turn round and wait until morning. With my heart thumping I called the harbour control on the VHF, but received no response. I continued on my way until I clearly saw the starboard hand light. I felt confident then to turn the corner. There, just ahead, a forest of masts confronted me!

With every fibre of my body I hoped that I would be able to find a spot for *Lucia*. As I crept past the fuel jetty, heading very slowly towards the marina, someone suddenly yelled at me. I turned and shouted to ask whether the man spoke English.

'Yes, yes. You come back now,' he called.

Carefully I turned *Lucia* around and headed for the fuel jetty. Just as I was coming alongside, I heard a woman's voice.

'Come on, Mo! We've been waiting days for you to arrive.' I was taken completely by surprise – who could possible know me here?

Despite my fatigue I managed to dock *Lucia* in a very seamanlike fashion. As I went forward to throw my lines to the willing hands ashore, I suddenly remembered where I had heard the voice of the woman who was calling to me. It was Joan, a radio ham. Although we had never met, I had heard her talking to the UK Maritime Net on several occasions during my voyage. She and her husband Dave helped me to secure *Lucia* under the watchful eye of the marina official.

It was so heartwarming to be met by such friendly, willing people as Joan and Dave. They had been listening to my radio transmissions with Paul and, having experienced similar conditions during their own approach to the island, knew that I had been having a tough time of it. They said they were determined to be on hand when I got in.

By now we had been joined by a police officer, demanding that the captain go ashore with the ship's papers. As I looked up at him my eyes came to rest on the gun in his hip holster. There was no way I was going to keep this man waiting! But Joan told him to give me a minute.

'She's on her own, you know,' she announced.

He stood there with his hands on his hips, staring down at me. 'You come as soon as you are ready,' he said in excellent English.

I invited Joan and Dave aboard and within seconds they were both hugging me warmly as if they had known me all my life. The three of us made sure *Lucia*'s lines were adjusted correctly before we went below to collect my papers. Joan advised me to take my time; she also gave me the wonderful news that the marina showers were open twenty-four hours a day. She understood only too well that the first thing most sailors want on arrival is a long hot shower. As I put my wash kit, clean clothes and Portuguese money into my bag, I thought that – unlike my arrival in Spain – this time I was well organised to go ashore.

Back in the cockpit once more, I was surprised to see the police officer still staring down at me. It was low tide and the leap ashore looked quite daunting, so I was relieved when Dave and the officer bent down to take my hands and hoisted me up the wall. As my feet touched dry land my legs wobbled weakly beneath me. I looked down in amazement: from being able to move like an orang-utan on board *Lucia*, on shore I was having great difficulty putting one foot in front of the other!

I followed the officer slowly into the building and

gratefully sat on a chair by his desk. As I removed my papers from my bag, my hands began to shake. He pushed a form towards me and asked me to complete it. When he saw that I was shaking he enquired whether I was nervous.

'No, I'm just very tired after being at sea for thirteen days. Everything feels a little strange at the moment'.

He took the form back from me. 'Maybe it would be better if I do this. You just answer the questions.'

He informed me that in the morning, when the immigration and customs offices were open, there would be more formalities to complete. He asked for the passports of the crew, and as I handed him my own passport I explained that I was sailing alone. He looked at me for such a long time that I began to feel quite embarrassed.

'This is not possible. In all my time as a Guarda Fiscal I have never seen a woman sailing alone.'

I had to stress many times that I was sorry but I really could not change the way it was. I was the captain, and I was definitely sailing alone.

He started to shake his head as he told me that once he had seen a boat with two women. Many times he had seen boats with one man. Never, never a boat with just one small woman. How was this possible?

I smiled at him as I replied, 'Sometimes even I wondered that, but *Lucia* is a fine boat and she was built specifically for me to sail alone.'

When the paperwork was completed, he took my hand in his and shook it firmly. 'It is with great pleasure I welcome you to my island. Is there anything you need?'

'I would like to telephone my family in England. Is there a payphone nearby?'

'You may use the office phone. It is on a meter, so you can pay when you have finished your calls.'

I was very touched by his kindness, as he not only

showed me to the phone but also insisted on placing a chair by it for me.

The first call I made was to Paul, who I hoped would still be waiting at his son's house. But Richard told me Paul had left half an hour before, as he felt sure I would not enter the harbour at night. I arranged to call again the following morning.

I then called Russel, who was over the moon that I had arrived safely. Colin was next, but all I got was his answering machine. Then I contacted my sister Sheila, who was shocked to hear my voice as she had talked to Paul an hour before and he had assured her I would not enter a strange harbour in the dark.

'Well, the sky was only dark blue as I entered – not pitch black. And anyway, I was desperate to wash my hair.'

She started to giggle.

'Oh, Mo, I've been so worried about you – but you sound great.'

'Well, apart from having wobbly legs and dirty hair, I feel on top of the world.'

Next I gave my parents a call, and I could almost see the relief in my mother's eyes when she heard my voice. My father, bless his heart, was so excited that I had arrived in the Azores.

'We heard from Paul that it's not been as eventful as your last voyage, but that it's not been easy either. Are you sure you're OK, dear?'

'I feel wonderful, Dad. Arriving in harbour seems to erase any problems I've encountered at sea.'

I explained that I would spend a few days in Sao Miguel before making my way to Faial, which was approximately thirty-six hours' sailing distance away.

Not needing to make any further calls until the morning, I paid the officer and thanked him for his kindness.

'The English version of my name is George. There is

no need for you to move your boat tonight – a place in the marina will be found for you in the morning. I will be here at seven tomorrow night, and I will be happy to help you with anything you may need.'

As I left his office, I was aglow with the sincerity of his words. Joan and Dave were waiting outside for me with a bottle of wine to celebrate my arrival. As we walked, my ears were assailed by the sound of loud music, laughter and voices. There must have been over 200 people clustered around the marina complex and I asked Joan if there was a party going on.

'No, this happens every night. It's a favourite place for the young people to collect. Don't worry – around midnight they start to disappear and it becomes very peaceful.'

Having been alone at sea for almost two weeks, I felt completely overwhelmed at the sight of so many people. Dave looked around for somewhere to sit and led us to a part of the wall overlooking the marina and away from the hubbub. We drank a toast to 'Free spirits' and I thanked them both for making my arrival a very special occasion. But I was only able to drink half a glass of wine, as even a small amount of alcohol was having a very intoxicating effect on my empty stomach. After a short time Joan showed me to the shower block where she insisted on running the water for me. Before she left, she promised to come to *Lucia* the next day to see how I was getting on.

When I removed my hat, I was appalled at the state of my hair. Apart from being really dirty, it had ballooned in volume from the effects of the salt spray. I shampooed and rinsed my hair four times before I felt satisfied it was clean. I must have spent a good hour in the shower. The wonderful, soothing effect of fresh water cascading over my hair and body was beyond description.

FAIAL: A TOUGH GOAL TO REACH

When I emerged from the shower block, the crowds had already begun to thin. The building that I had thought was just a bar also housed a café. As by now I was feeling very hungry, I squeezed through the remaining people to the counter to enquire if I was too late to order some food. They could only offer me a pizza, but at that moment a pizza sounded delicious. I sat at an outside table waiting for it to arrive, feeling as if I had just descended from outer space. The sights and sounds of the people around me had a distant, dreamlike quality. When my meal was set before me, it smelt wonderful. Having eaten only cream crackers and digestive biscuits for the last thirty-six hours it was not surprising that I drooled over each mouthful. But before I was halfway through I was full to bursting. I made my way back to *Lucia*, waving to George as I went, feeling a very happy, peaceful woman.

As I slipped beneath the clean sheets I had put on my bed, I hoped that this time I would sleep until morning. However, it was not to be – the longest period I managed was one and a half hours. But my insomnia did not trouble me at all; each time I awoke, I lay in a contented glow until I drifted off to sleep once more.

CHAPTER TEN

THIRD TIME LUCKY

At 6a.m., with the sun streaming through the ports, I
got up, longing to see what my new surroundings
looked like in daylight. I sat on deck drinking a cup of
tea, delighted at how clean and fresh the harbour and
marina were. As I gazed around at the white buildings
sparkling in the early morning sunshine my heart filled
with joy. Sao Miguel might not have been the exact
island I set out for, but I was determined not to let that
spoil the enjoyment of arrival.

Since the immigration and customs office would not
be open until 9a.m., I took myself ashore to indulge in
another shower. I returned feeling squeaky-clean and
was delighted to see *Kite* tied up alongside *Lucia*. Mark
and Polly turned out to be a super young couple and,
although they were tired, they were as excited as me to
be safely in harbour. We agreed to meet the next day
and explore the town together.

I went below to start the marathon task of organising
Lucia for harbour life. On one of my many trips to
transfer equipment to the cockpit, I noticed several people
standing on the dock looking down at us. One man

called out to me, asking if I remembered him. I looked at him long and hard but had to confess I did not.

'We met in La Coruna – I was on the Irish boat moored opposite you.'

I apologised as I shook his hand.

'My brother, our skipper, has sent me to ask you to join us for coffee. As we plan to leave for Ireland very soon, would it be possible for you to come with me now?'

Feeling happy to take a break from my labours, I agreed to go with him. As we walked together towards his yacht, I did indeed recognise it from La Coruna. When we got to the Irish boat the skipper said he had something to confess to me. I was completely flabbergasted when he dropped to his knees and begged me to forgive him.

'Whatever for?'

'I did you a great wrong when I met you in La Coruna and heard of the dreadful problems you'd had during your first passage – I was convinced you'd never set sail again. After you left the marina bar, while others were singing your praises I proclaimed that it wouldn't be long before your boat would be up for sale and you would return to England, never to venture on the high seas again. Yet here you are as large as life, having sailed alone halfway across the ocean. Do you have it in your heart to forgive me?'

I could not help laughing as I helped him to his feet. I assured him that he was not alone in not taking me seriously, and that of course I would forgive him. While I drank my coffee I told him I remembered the odd look he had given me the last time we had met, and now I knew the reason why. I went on to explain that ridicule had been rife from the moment I had decided on my new way of life, that I had never expected it to be easy and I was certainly not going to let one gale stop me living a life that had surpassed my wildest dreams.

On my way back to *Lucia* I stopped off to phone Paul and told him what a wonderful welcome I had received. He was a little concerned about my entering the harbour at night, but I tried to reassure him by explaining how straightforward the entrance was.

'Anyway, I just had to come in to wash my hair,' I stated. There were a few seconds of silence and then, 'Of course you did,' he cheekily replied.

I collected my ship's papers and went to the relevant offices to complete the necessary paperwork. The Azores belong to Portugal, and the Portuguese, unlike the Spanish, have a great liking for red tape. It took almost an hour to obtain the official stamps on the forms I had to fill out, in quadruplicate. It was quite wearing going from office to office, each time having to convince the staff that I really was sailing alone. There was a moment when I thought the immigration officer was going to come and tear *Lucia* apart in the hope of finding a hidden crew. As the last stamp was applied to my forms, I was instructed to report to the marina office at noon when I would be appointed a berth.

As I stepped back aboard *Lucia*, Joan – who had met me on my arrival with her husband Dave – came over to see if she could help me. She was terrific – nothing was too much trouble for her and before long *Lucia* was looking very orderly. After we had had a well-earned cup of tea, we went to the marina office. A young lady who said she was delighted to meet the English woman who was sailing alone greeted me. Word was getting round.

'Never before have I met such a brave woman,' she said, grasping my hand. She gave me a pile of brochures which she thought I might find useful and appointed me a berth on the end of a pontoon, which proved very easy to take *Lucia* alongside.

Before I left the fuel dock, I filled *Lucia*'s tank with

much-needed diesel and then, with Joan aboard, gently motored to our appointed position. Dave was standing by to take my lines, and very quickly *Lucia* was secured to the pontoon. After eating a light lunch in the cockpit I went below, finished recording my log and then fell into a deep sleep. When I awoke three hours later I felt wonderful.

That evening I went for a short walk around the marina and eventually came to the yacht club restaurant. It was extremely upmarket and I wondered if I would be allowed in. I felt a little nervous as I walked towards the bar and asked for the menu. The waiter informed me that it was a buffet and I could help myself to as much as I wanted. The price he quoted seemed very reasonable, and I made my way through to the dining room where I gazed in disbelief at the buffet tables laden with a huge variety of meat, fish, vegetables and salad. I was so hungry for fresh food that by the time I sat down my table was covered in little plates, each containing a sample of everything on offer.

As I slowly ate my way through this Aladdin's cave of dishes savouring every mouthful, I looked round at the other diners. My eyes kept coming back to two ladies who looked as far removed from sailors as you could get. They were dressed in expensive outfits and one of them was heavily bedecked in jewellery. I looked away in embarrassment, and hoped they would not think I was staring. When I looked up again, one of them waved at me and yelled, 'Honey, are you British?'

'Yes.'

'Why don't you come over here and join us?'

As I made my way towards their table, the lady who had invited me over said, 'You must be Maureen.'

'How on earth do you know my name?'

'Honey, *everybody* here knows who you are!'

I sat down stunned. They introduced themselves as

Brenda and Winnie, both Americans, who lived on the island for six months of the year. My two new acquaintances may have been senior citizens, but they were very young at heart and I found them great fun to be with. I did my best to answer the multitude of questions they fired at me. Before we parted company, Brenda made me promise to visit her and use her tub whenever I wanted. Winnie insisted on giving me a guided tour of the island and we arranged to meet the day after next.

That night, as I lay in my bed thinking about the day's events, I felt terrific. Surrounded by people showing me exceptional warmth and kindness, I was on a real high. I just hoped that my bubble would not burst too soon.

The next morning I met Mark and Polly as arranged and we embarked on a grand tour of the town. It was impossible to cover it all in one morning, but what we did see impressed us greatly. The town was built on a gently ascending hill; the main street facing the harbour was quite modern but as we turned up one of the side roads, we were delighted to emerge amongst the beautiful buildings of the old city. Tiny bars were dotted about everywhere and even early in the morning, men were gathered drinking strange coloured liquid from small glasses, earnestly discussing the topic of the day. As we made our way up and along, a square would open up before us, housing an impressive church or government building. We eventually found the market but realised that we would have to time our next visit very early to purchase the best of the produce on offer.

Back on *Lucia*, I spent the rest of the day writing letters and catching up on odd jobs. I was still concerned about my alternator and had discussed the problem with Mark, who had promised he would have a look and see if he could solve it for me.

That evening I had a visit from George, the Guarda

Fiscal, who was thrilled to have a guided tour of *Lucia*. I told him how much I was looking forward to seeing more of his beautiful island and he told me a lot about the history of Sao Miguel. Before he left he made me promise I would not hesitate to ask him if I required anything during my stay.

Winnie took me on a grand tour of the southern end of the island. As we made our way inland I could not help myself continually exclaiming at the abundance of beautiful plants. The hedges of wild hydrangeas were stunning. We visited the amazing Terra Nostra Park, where I bathed in a pool fed by a natural hot spring. I stood for a long time massaging my neck and back against the gushing flow of the spring, while gazing at the many exotic flowers and trees surrounding the pool. When I emerged my skin was covered in a thin film of iron and mineral deposits. My body felt soothed and revitalised.

The pungent smell of sulphur stung my nose and eyes as we wandered through the area of Furnas, admiring the thermal springs and boiling mud pools. We stopped to buy loaves of round flat bread, baked by the village women in the hot volcanic earth. When toasted, the bread tasted like a delicious version of the English crumpet. As our day came to an end I found it difficult to express my gratitude to Winnie for the treasures she had shown me. She assured me the pleasure she had derived throughout the day was all the thanks she needed.

During the following few days I was swept up in a fever of social activity. Mark and Polly had met a super man called Jo, who had been born on the island, emigrated to Canada and was now enjoying his annual holiday. Jo and his cousin Tony insisted on taking the three of us to see the northern end of the island. We had a wonderful day visiting some spectacular sites including the Caldeira das Sete Cidades. The twin lakes formed at the base of the Calderia (volcanic crater) are called Largoa Verde (Green Lake) and Largoa Azul (Blue Lake) and are divided by a bridge.

We spent a little time resting at the lakesides before driving up the winding road to the top of the Caldeira, frequently stopping to admire the incredible scenery. Jo told us of the romantic legend attributed to the lakes. 'A beautiful princess, with a green and a blue eye, created the lakes with her tears, when she was parted forever, from her lover.' The other more likely theory is that dissolved minerals or algae have caused the vivid emerald and sapphire colours of the lakes.

I was also a guest at numerous dinner parties in local restaurants or on board other people's yachts. To thank all these people for their generous hospitality, two nights before I left, I held a party on *Lucia* to coincide with a surprise birthday celebration for Joan. At one minute past midnight I presented Joan with a candlelit birthday cake, and her eyes filled with tears of happiness as we sang 'Happy Birthday'. When I awoke the next morning, I found a huge bag of avocados and a hand of bananas in the cockpit. These were a present from a couple called George and Eleanor, who have a plantation on the island. I shared these goodies among my friends on the other yachts, and we all agreed that memories of Sao Miguel would stay with us for a long time.

On 17 July I was delighted to find that conditions would be just right by the following day for my short hop to the island of Faial. Although I was reluctant to leave Sao Miguel, I wanted to arrive in Horta harbour with at least one day in hand so that I could rest before the start of the centenary celebrations. Mark and Polly had come to the same decision, and we agreed to set off together the next morning. I phoned Paul to tell him of my plans and we arranged to try and make radio contact on the evening of the 18th.

I dashed to the supermarket to top up my supplies, collected my laundry and then prepared *Lucia* to set sail. Mark and Jo, who was an aircraft engineer, had replaced my alternator bracket and fan belts. Jo felt this was only a temporary solution, however, as he was sure my engine had come out of alignment. He advised me to get Paul to give it some serious attention when we met in Lisbon. I checked out with customs and immigration and then spent some time saying farewell to my many new-found friends. Brenda and Winnie had decided to fly to Faial to take part in the centenary celebrations. Brenda assured me that they knew how to throw a good party there. In past years she had been a regular visitor on Faial, and she was looking forward to introducing me to her many friends on the island.

Soon after I awoke the next morning I started receiving visits from people who wanted to wish me well. Jerry, from *Nell Gwen*, who was also a single-handed sailor, helped me with my lines. By 9.30a.m. I was slowly motoring out of the marina and flutters of excitement were building within me. With a distance of no more than 160 miles or so to go I was fairly confident, God willing, that this, my third attempt to sail to Faial, would prove successful. Mark and Polly were ahead of me, and by the time I reached the outer harbour *Kite*'s impressive tan sails were filling with wind. I raised *Lucia*'s sails, set her on course for Faial, and with a fresh south-westerly wind we were soon speeding along at five knots. The exhilaration of sailing in almost perfect conditions was unbelievable.

Within a few hours I lost sight of *Kite*. My last contact with Mark was at 2p.m., when he called me on the VHF radio. I was able to report that all was well on board *Lucia* and we were enjoying an excellent sail. It came as a complete surprise, then, when an hour later I was extremely seasick. As the wind strength increased I deep reefed the main sail and furled half the jib away. Thankfully Joshua, my wind vane self-steering, was holding *Lucia* on course and I was able to rest between the violent bouts of sickness.

That evening I was unable to make contact with Paul. I returned to the cockpit as quickly as possible because being down below, even for a few moments, aggravated my condition. I was shocked at how weak I felt so early in my voyage, and could only think that six days in harbour had not given me enough time to recover from my previous passage. I made up my mind that when I got to Faial I would stay for a considerable time in order to build up my strength before setting off for Lisbon. The night passed in a blur of keeping watch and trying to sleep. During the early hours of the morning the wind began to ease. I shook out the reefs and set *Lucia* on the best point of sail, but our progress was nowhere near as swift as on the previous day. At the present rate, the trip would take me much longer than anticipated.

Still unable to shake off the seasickness, I felt it would be unwise to attempt radio contact at 8a.m. I decided to venture below only when I needed to visit the heads, and over the following few hours I rested as much as possible in the cockpit. The highlight of the day came late in the afternoon when the dolphins arrived. The sight of these beautiful creatures lifted my spirits, and by early evening I felt well enough to contact Paul. But the conditions were dreadful and, although I knew he was there, I could not make out a single word. Eventually I managed to relay my position, send him 88s and say all was well on board.

With the darkness came very confused seas – *Lucia* was pounding into waves that were rising by the hour. I replaced the reefs in the sails, concerned that maybe a gale was brewing, then sat in the cockpit with my sleeping bag wrapped around me and tried to picture the weather map I had seen in Sao Miguel. As the image formed in my mind, I was sure there had been nothing to indicate bad weather and told myself to stop worrying.

As the night progressed the wind began to drop, but not the seas. I shook out the reefs, trimmed the sails and tried everything I could to maintain our speed. This activity sapped at my meagre strength, and within seconds I was hanging my head over the guardrail. With nothing left in my stomach to offer Neptune, the next few minutes were a dreadful experience. After that I sipped a little water and sucked on a boiled sweet, throwing the paper overboard. At 4a.m., having repeated this exercise many times, I fell into an exhausted sleep.

Suddenly I felt somebody's hands around my eyes and I heard Paul's voice, telling me it was time to get up. He was urging me to get on with the sailing.

'There's something I want to show you.'

I really could not believe that he was so close to me. As I turned I clearly saw his face and felt him kiss me on my cheek, leaving it moist from his lips. He was telling me off, saying that he had been following me for some time and that I had left a trail of sweet papers behind me. He helped me up from where I was lying, put his arm around me and kissed me on my cheek again.

'Look,' he said, 'this is what I wanted to show you.'

There in front of me was the island of Pico engulfed in sunlight. It was the most beautiful sight I had ever seen. I felt Paul's strength and love flowing through me as he guided me to the helm, and then he was gone.

I really do not know how to explain this phenomenal event. All I can say is that when I looked around to see where he had disappeared to I was indeed standing at the helm, and there on the horizon was the magnificent sight of the island of Pico aglow in the dawn sunshine. I looked at my watch: it was just 5a.m. I stood for a while gazing at Pico as I tried to gather my wits. Feeling perplexed but very happy, I nibbled on some biscuits and then set about the work in hand. Finding it difficult to make four knots under sail alone, I started the engine and we motor sailed for some hours. As we edged our way past Pico, I took some photographs as clouds brushed her mountainous peak.

When I called Paul at 8a.m. he came through loud and clear. After giving given him my position I asked him what he had been doing at 5a.m.

'Why?' came the response.

'I just need to know. Were you sound asleep?'

'No. I was lying in bed, wondering where you were and wishing there was some way I could help you.'

I decided I would wait until we were face to face before I told him of my incredible experience.

Paul went on to say that people would think I was really flash, arriving on the day of Joshua Slocum's centenary. I hoped he was wrong, as that had not been my intention at all.

As *Lucia* and I motor sailed past Pico, Faial came into view. I could hardly believe that at last, on 20 July, I would arrive at the island I had originally set out for on 19 May. Excitement washed over me like a tidal wave as I went forward to prepare my lines. Ahead of me, what appeared to be a large brown box was floating on the water. I looked more closely and was delighted to see that it was a huge turtle. I watched, mesmerised, as we slowly passed each other.

We were now within sight of the harbour wall. I dropped my mainsail, went up on deck and tied it neatly, then returned to the cockpit and started to furl the jib – which immediately jammed. I turned *Lucia* away from the harbour towards open water, and went forward to see what the problem was. I could see several riding turns on the drum housing the furling line. I must have relaxed the tension on the line the last time I unfurled it. With a great deal of struggling I managed to release one of the turns, but no matter how I tried I could not free the others. I decided I would have to enter the harbour without furling the sail, confident that there would be no problem as long as I made sure the sheet was flying free, allowing the wind to spill from the sail. I called the harbour radio to ask permission to enter, explaining that I had a minor problem with my furling gear. I offered to anchor in the outer harbour if they preferred, but they were happy about this and instructed me to enter.

Suddenly Mark's voice came over the VHF: 'Mo, don't worry. Polly and I will be standing by on the dock to take your lines. Take it easy and you'll be fine.'

At 1550 hours, with my lines and fenders in place, I slowly made my approach. Rounding the harbour wall, I edged towards the reception dock. There was a large yacht moored to one end, and I lined *Lucia* up to slip in behind it. I could see Mark and Polly standing on the dock with three other people. I went forward and threw the centre cleat line to Mark, only to watch it slip through his hands. By the time I had retrieved the line the wind had pushed *Lucia* away from the dock. I called out that I would come round again.

As I carefully turned *Lucia* around in a big circle, I was confronted by a fleet of sailing dinghies with small children at the helms. They were heading in every direction and I had to concentrate really hard to avoid them. On my second approach to the dock I decided it would in fact be easier to moor alongside the large yacht rather than behind it and shouted my intentions to Mark. I gently made my way forward as Mark and the others leaped aboard the moored yacht. I had to be very careful; raised on davits on its stern was a dinghy with an outboard engine sticking out a long way towards my bow. One of my helpers leaned over and pushed *Lucia*'s forward shroud clear of the outboard.

What happened next was totally confusing; as I was handing my lines to the other helpers, crew from the yacht to which I was trying to moor were rushing around yelling. One of them was shaking his fist at me and, even though the words he was screaming at me were in Spanish, a language I do not speak, it was obvious they were not of a pleasant nature. Mark told me to ignore him, while the man who had pushed me clear of the protruding dinghy said in very clear English that he was the marina manager and *Lucia* could stay exactly where she was.

Two of the people who had come to my assistance suddenly leaped aboard *Lucia* and started hugging me. It turned out to be Corie and William, a lovely Dutch couple whom I had met in La Coruna. In the general melee I did not recognise them at first, then as I was returning their hugs, my attention was distracted by the behaviour of one of the Spanish men. He was jumping up and down on the deck of his boat, screaming at me. I walked towards him in the hope of calming him down and finding out what the problem was, but a man with a strong Irish accent who introduced himself as Henry quickly intervened.

'I'm in the insurance business,' he warned me, 'and I advise you to be very careful what you say to this man. No way should you even mention the word sorry – you've done nothing wrong.'

I tried hard with gestures and signs to placate the Spanish man, but it only seemed to have the effect of making him even more angry with me.

Another of the Spanish crew, who spoke English, told me that I had hit their yacht with great force and caused extensive damage. I could hardly believe my ears – I knew damn well I had not hit the yacht. I turned to the others to ask if I was at fault, and they all agreed with me. At that point I should have been the one to get angry, but I decided it just was not worth it. I walked away feeling very tired and upset.

The marina manager, José, asked me to collect my ship's papers and follow him into the office. When we were alone he told me that the Spanish yacht had been nothing but trouble since its arrival. To begin with its crew had anchored in the centre of the harbour, making it extremely difficult for other traffic to pass. Once against the reception dock they refused to move to a marina berth unless the manager accepted responsibility for any damage incurred while they did so. This was all very odd, and I wondered what their game was.

José appointed me a berth and hoped I would enjoy my visit in spite of the unpromising start. Back on *Lucia*, Corie and William said they would stay aboard and help me with my lines when we got to the berth. But when Mark and Polly stepped on to the Spanish yacht to cast *Lucia* off, the crew refused to let me leave until I paid for the damage they said I had caused. Feeling very intimidated, I promised that if they would release my lines, I would return in an hour to discuss the matter further. As we motored to my allotted spot William and Corie reassured me that, no matter what the Spanish crew said, I certainly had not collided with their yacht. I felt dreadful and began to doubt my manoeuvring skills. Until, that is, I brought *Lucia* into a very tight spot between another yacht and the pontoon without a single hitch.

As soon as I was left alone I sat down and tried to gather my thoughts. I decided the first thing I needed was a shower. After that, a little revived, I made my way to the Spanish yacht, determined to resolve this unpleasant matter. From the stern they were flying the

Union Jack, something else which I found very strange. Once on board I asked the names of the two men confronting me: to add to the confusion, they were both called Carlos. By now Carlos the skipper seemed to have calmed down. Carlos the interpreter asked me to sit down.

The first thing the skipper wanted to know was the name of my insurance company, so that he could make a claim for the damage I had done.

'What damage?' I asked.

They took me on deck and began to show me areas of damage that from the rust stains were obviously quite old. When I pointed this out, the skipper began to get very angry and demanded I pay the sum of seventeen thousand dollars.

'Surely you mean escudos?'

'No, he wants American dollars,' replied the interpreter.

I looked at them both and almost laughed, but instead fixed them with a very serious look. 'This is getting ridiculous. For a start I did not cause the damage to your vessel, and even if I had seventeen thousand dollars would be a totally unrealistic figure.'

Carlos the skipper started to yell at me again. Carlos the interpreter told me he was demanding that I tell him the name of my insurance company. When I still refused the skipper leaped up and down, insulting my gender and my ability to sail in very graphic terms. Then he threatened to impound *Lucia* unless I paid him immediately. I felt very browbeaten as I tried without success to convince him that I had not collided with his boat. Eventually I told him I would get hold of the people who had assisted me on my arrival and ask them to give their opinion, which I hoped would settle the matter.

As I stepped ashore Carlos the interpreter followed me, which made me feel extremely anxious. He started talking to me in hushed tones.

'I feel very sad for you, but Carlos, my skipper, is not a man to ignore. I know him very well. He always gets his own way, and it would be better for you to pay what he asks now. If not, he will make you suffer.'

I dug deep to find some courage and turned to him.

'Stop following me,' I ordered. 'Go back to your skipper and tell him I will return with the people who were there when I arrived, to prove to him that I did not cause the damage to his boat.'

As I hurried away from him, I hoped he had not seen how afraid I was. Within half an hour, with the five people concerned in tow, I returned to the Spanish yacht. Henry took it on himself to be spokesperson and tried to settle things, but in vain. Tempers became very short, so we told the skipper we would give him until the morning to come to his senses, and left.

CHAPTER ELEVEN

HURRICANE TANIA

That evening the people of Faial were staging a classical concert as part of the Slocum centenary celebrations. Mark and Polly insisted that I have a meal with them, after which they wanted to escort me to the concert. When I explained that all I wanted to do was return to *Lucia* to rest, they told me I simply had to attend the concert. Did I not realise that I was the only Spray to have made it to the island, and that I had arrived within forty minutes of the time of Slocum's arrival one hundred years before me? After they had given me a few moments to digest this news, I agreed that it would be most ungracious of me just to go to bed.

I felt a little stronger after I had eaten, and before going on to the concert I telephoned Paul. He sounded a little down and explained that, although he did not want to upset me, there was something he had to tell me. It had been playing on his mind for some time and he felt he had to discuss it with me now. My heart leaped into my throat as I asked him to continue.

'Mo, I'm not going to be ready to set sail for Lisbon in September. Richard is ill and I've been spending a great deal of time with him. He needs me, Mo, so there's no way I can leave him for a long time to go off sailing around the world.'

As I tried to get my head around what he was saying, he asked me if I would consider leaving *Lucia* in the Azores and flying back to the UK so that we could be together for a short time. I told him to give me some time to think things through – that he should not worry about setting sail and of course he should do all he could to help his son through his illness.

He apologised again for unloading his problems on me as soon as I got into harbour and asked how things had gone. I told him about my encounter with the Spanish skipper, which only set him off on another line of worry.

'It's OK, darling,' I assured him. 'I have plenty of support here, and in the morning I'm sure I'll be able to sort this problem out.'

'Mo, this is so strange. How much of *Sailing Alone Around the World* have you read?'

I was a little confused and asked, 'What's that got to do with my fight with the Spanish yacht?'

'Have you got to the part when Joshua Slocum arrived in Horta?'

'No. Why?'

'Well, he had a pilot on board to enter the harbour and they too encountered problems. They sank a small barge which, if memory serves me right, was Spanish!'

As I walked with Mark and Polly towards the beautiful old building where the concert was being held, a thought crossed my mind. Was history trying to repeat itself! I decided to read the rest of Joshua's book as soon as possible.

Thankfully, the evening was a great success. There were many dignitaries in attendance and I was given a very warm welcome. The music was excellent and I found it very soothing. Unfortunately I was very tired and at one point I almost fell asleep, but, with Polly's help, I did manage to last out until the end. When I eventually got to bed I wondered if it would be possible for me to sleep with so many unsolved problems on my mind. I reminded myself that nothing lasts forever, and that this blip in my now otherwise blissful lifestyle would soon be over.

The next thing I knew it was 6a.m., and I had slept soundly all night. I felt so much clearer about the events of the previous day and was determined to put the Spanish skipper firmly in his place. At about nine I called on Henry and told him of the plan I had worked out. He agreed with my proposed course of action and insisted that he and his wife accompany me. They both spoke Spanish and he felt it was essential that I had witnesses to whatever occurred.

When the two Carloses were in front of me, I asked the interpreter to translate my words verbatim. He spoke to the skipper for a few moments, and while he was doing so Henry called me to one side.

'Mo, from what they are saying, I'm pretty sure the skipper does understand English. Also, I've just looked at the stern of this yacht. Some of the damage they attributed to you yesterday and said was beyond repair is no longer evident!'

I walked slowly back to the skipper and spoke to him firmly.

'Carlos, would you look at me please.'

'I no speak English.'

'I think you do. I will speak very slowly, as I don't want you to miss a single word.' He turned away from me, so I went and stood directly in front of him.

'Carlos, yesterday I was very tired and you tried to intimidate me and extract money from me under false pretences.'

'*I no speak English.*'

As anger built within me I stared directly into his eyes, lowered my voice and again spoke slowly and carefully.

'Carlos, you are a very, very small man.' I held my hands up in front of him with my thumbs and fore-fingers an inch apart. Then I threw my arms wide apart. 'But a big, big shit!'

In clear English he began to curse me, but I interrupted him and repeated my words and actions. This time I beat my chest and raised my voice as I spoke.

'I may only be a little woman, but I am very strong of heart and mind. You cannot intimidate me. *I will never, never pay you any money.*'

Both Carloses screamed abuse at me and the skipper yelled in my face.

'*I will get you and your boat.*'

'Really? In that case I am going right now to report you to the police and sue you for demanding money with threatening behaviour.'

I turned and marched away from him, with Henry and his wife following. When they caught up Henry congratulated me, but his wife was worried that I was upset.

'I'm a little shaky,' I confessed, 'but I feel great.'

We stopped off at a café, had some coffee and enquired where the police station was. As I collected my thoughts I realised I did not have the name of the Spanish yacht. I ran down to the dock, only to discover it had disappeared. José, the marina manager, was standing there with a big smile on his face. He took my hand and shook it vigorously.

'The minute you were out of sight, they left!' he said triumphantly. 'We've been trying to get them to leave for days and now you have solved our problem for us. Don't worry – they will not be allowed to enter harbour again.'

LONE VOYAGER

I returned to the café and told Henry and his wife the good news. While we were still discussing the Spanish yacht's hasty retreat Mark, Polly, William and Corie rushed in, shouting at the tops of their voices that the yacht had disappeared. Our laughter filled the café as Henry told them what had occurred that morning.

As the laughter faded, I cast my eyes over my surroundings. Here I was in Peter's Café Sport, the most famous meeting-place for sailors in the world. I gazed at the walls and ceiling, which were covered in sailing mementoes from thousands of visiting yachts: there were photographs, flags and pieces of sail bearing the signatures of captains and crew. I was completely immersed in the incredible atmosphere when I felt a hand on my shoulder.

'Are you OK, Mo?'

'Yes, Polly, I'm just trying to take all this in. It's hard to believe that at last I've really arrived and I'm not just dreaming.'

In the corner of the room sat an elderly man – Peter Azevedo, the café proprietor. Back in England I had listened to so many stories about Peter, who has a wonderful reputation for looking after yachtsmen. I was told that nothing was too much trouble for him. I walked across the room and Peter, who spoke excellent English, welcomed me warmly and told me he was sure there was some post for me. I collected my mail and arranged to meet the others later that evening at the Club Naval Da Horta for a special reception to honour Joshua Slocum. Then I made my way back to *Lucia*.

As I looked down from the top of the harbour wall, I was surprised to see a film crew surrounding her. Having had more than enough excitement for one day, I decided to go for a walk until they had left. I wandered around the marina enthralled as I looked at the paintings decorating the harbour walls. Some were superb works of art, depicting yachts, whales, birds, flags and extravagant designs. Others were simply names and dates, but each one told its own story. Horta has been a Mecca for yachtspeople for a century, and it has long been a tradition that it is unlucky to leave without painting a picture on the walls.

Back aboard *Lucia* I settled down to read my letters, after which I fell into a contented sleep. I awoke just in time to get ready for the reception. Having gone to such an effort to arrive in Faial in time for the celebrations I did not want to miss a moment of them. On my way to the Club Naval I bumped into John, a friend of Brenda's whom I had met the previous evening. While we were talking a car came to a halt in front of us. Out stepped a very well-dressed gentleman and I found myself being introduced to Renato Luis Pereira Leal, the President of Horta! He kissed me on both cheeks and congratulated me on my achievement. Before taking his leave, he said he hoped to have a first-hand account of my adventure very soon.

The Club Naval was brimming with people and I found myself being whisked from group to group. I was already feeling overwhelmed with all the attention I was receiving when the president of the club presented me with their burgee, saying that they would be honoured if I flew it from *Lucia*'s mast. I assured him the honour was all mine and that I would fly the burgee with pride. I later learnt that *Lucia* was featured on the Azorean television news that evening.

The next two days were full of excitement and events such as yacht races, exhibitions, tours and talks. The grand finale was an excellent party held at the Club Naval, where Renato Leal greeted me as if we were old friends. He was very complimentary and told me how impressed he was that I had sailed alone to his island, bringing the spirit of Joshua Slocum's epic voyage alive.

He asked me if it had been difficult to get the timing right to within a few minutes of Joshua Slocum's arrival time one hundred years before. When I explained that my timing was pure luck, I felt sure he did not believe me. Renato introduced me to Raiel Martin, the captain of a visiting sail training ship from Uruguay, the *Captain Miranda*. Raiel, who looked very smart and impressive in his white uniform, invited me to join Renato the next day for a guided tour of his ship.

That evening after leaving the party I went to Peter's Café to try to telephone my son Colin. A group of musicians from the *Captain Miranda* had set up their instruments in the corner of the café and began to play just as I got through. Their music was extremely hypnotic, and as it rose in volume my whole body began to vibrate.

'Where did you say you were, Mum?' Colin asked.

'Horta. It's in the Azores, darling,' I yelled.

'Are you sure, Mum? It sounds more like South America to me.'

It soon became impossible to carry on with our conversation, and as I replaced the receiver Colin's last words were ringing in my ears.

'Sounds great, Mum. Maybe I should fly out and have a holiday with you now!'

My visit to the *Captain Miranda* the next day was a wonderful experience. I was shown into the captain's cabin and, after accepting a drink, I was escorted by a young crew member, Daniel Bellagamba, on a tour that took over an hour. I was very impressed by the pristine condition of this beautiful ship with its exquisite Art Nouveau décor. I rejoined Raiel and Renato for a farewell drink before stepping ashore to await the ship's departure. Renato and I watched spellbound as the entire crew lined the decks from the tip of the bowsprit to the stern – even the ship's dog was present.

I must have got a little carried away by the spirit of the moment because I suddenly called to the young man who had been my guide, asking if I could have his cap as a memento. Without hesitation he removed it and threw it to me. Renato and I were I enthralled as this beautiful ship slipped smoothly out of the harbour. I happily accepted a lift back to *Lucia* in Renato's official car and asked him if he would like to see what a yacht at the other end of the scale was like, so he spent the following hour aboard with me on *Lucia*. Before he left he wrote a very flattering entry in my visitors' book.

Over the next few weeks I met a great many people, for every day yachts were arriving and departing to and from destinations all over the world. I was in regular contact with Paul and, although I was longing to see him, I could not have chosen a nicer location to pass the time until we were together again. We had agreed that, as soon as he felt happy that his son was getting better, instead of me flying to England he would fly to Horta and have a well-deserved holiday.

As I whiled away my time resting and recuperating from my recent voyages and the centenary celebrations. I would often walk to a spot not far from the harbour, the top of Monte de Guia. As I stood at the rim of this volcanic crater, I would stare out across the Atlantic Ocean mystified. Did I really sail all that way alone? It took a long time for me to comprehend that I had achieved such a big part of my dream. I now had the time to read *Sailing Alone Around the World*, and found it uncanny that I was encountering many of the experiences that Joshua had written about. One part in particular sent a shiver of recognition down my spine. 'Early on the morning of 20 July I saw Pico looming above the clouds on the starboard bow. Lower lands burst forth as the sun burned away the morning fog.' As I read his wonderful book I developed a very deep respect for Joshua's remarkable courage, along with a strong attachment to him.

I had been in Horta for approximately four weeks when *Windweaver* sailed into the harbour from the Caribbean. Just one look at Erik and I could clearly see the Viking in him, and Daphne's French accent was beguiling. Erik and Daphne both talented artists with the gentlest of natures, soon become like brother and sister to me. I met many like-minded people in the Azores, some of whom will remain lifetime friends. During August, when Faial celebrates the *Semar de Mar* (Sea Week), I was invited to crew for many yachts taking part in the races. Marijka, skipper of one yacht, got together an all-ladies' crew. She and her five other crew members lived on the island, and I was delighted when she asked me to join them. We did not do very well in the race, but we had so much fun that it did not worry any of us in the least. I regarded it as a great honour when the president of the yacht club asked me if I would present some of the awards afterwards.

As time progressed and the thrill of arrival faded, I settled down to a very comfortable way of life while I waited for Paul to arrive. He was booked on a flight in mid-September and planned to stay with me for four weeks. September seemed to take forever to arrive, but I was only too aware that once Paul appeared our time together would fly by.

On the day I was to meet him at the airport I felt as if I was sixteen years old. I had changed my clothes more times in a few hours than I normally did in a month. With one hour to go before I had to leave, I was still undecided. I had pulled almost every garment I possessed out of my wardrobe and eventually made a decision. Then I got all hot and bothered as I crammed the discarded clothes back into the cupboard. When I finally set off, my heart and stomach were all of a flutter and my mind was full of doubts. What if the moment he set eyes on me he had a change of heart? How would I cope with seeing the doubt in his eyes? I felt sick with anxiety and made frequent visits to the ladies.

The airport is very small and the open viewing platform overlooks the runaway. As Paul stepped from the plane I held my breath. He was looking intently at the crowd of waiting people, and then he spotted me. The smile that spread across his wonderful face was full of love, and when we embraced my doubts disappeared in an instant. The next four weeks passed in pure joy with the growing knowledge that time and distance were no threat to our relationship.

Paul, Erik and Daphne liked each other on sight, and when the four of us were not putting the world to rights in Peter's Café we were exploring the island. Paul, being the practical man he is, also found time to check *Lucia* over and make any repairs and adjustments he felt were necessary. The day he flew back to England was very emotional. Paul was the last person to board the plane, and as we kissed goodbye tears were flowing freely down the cheeks of both of us. He planned to return at Christmas for a short time, and I hung on to that comfort as I watched his plane take off and disappear until all that I could see was a tiny speck in the sky.

I returned to *Lucia*, moored as she was in an ideal spot with an excellent view of the island of Pico. Some weeks later, on 1 November, I was up at dawn admiring the first sight of snow on the top of Pico. I was taking a photo when I noticed a strange cloud formation take shape over her peak. The sea was oily calm and I was enjoying the peace of it all when I noticed José, the marina manager, rushing down the pontoons towards *Lucia* with a look of great concern on his face. During my time in Faial the marina officials had issued many false alarms of approaching hurricanes. This time, however,

José assured me, there would be no escape: Hurricane Tania was on her way and I must do all I could to prepare *Lucia* for the onslaught.

Windweaver was moored next to *Lucia*, but Erik and Daphne were staying ashore looking after a friend's house. I telephoned them to pass on José's warning, and Erik said he would be along later to prepare *Windweaver*. On my way to the marina office to look at the weather map I met some other friends. Ron and his mother Diana were British and they were living aboard their World War II motor sailing yacht *Montana* moored along the wall behind *Lucia*. Although at first none of us was over-concerned, we decided to take the matter very seriously when we saw that the weather map did indeed show the possibility of something nasty approaching. Ron, bless his heart, offered to lay out my fifty-pound fisherman anchor astern of *Lucia*. In fact he spent most of the morning in his dinghy laying out extra anchors for many of the yachts moored in the harbour.

I remembered Paul persuading me to buy my fisherman anchor. We were at a boat jumble and he asked me if I could try to lift the huge anchor above my knees.

'Whatever for?'

'Well, if you can lift it that high now, you'll be able to lift it a whole lot higher in a hurricane!'

He wasn't wrong. When the time came, with a fair amount of adrenaline pumping through my veins I lifted that anchor, with chain and rope attached, clear of the guardrail and handed it to Ron who was waiting along-side in his dinghy. I asked Ron if he could also take my strongest braided line, which I had attached to a winch on *Lucia*'s stern, across the harbour to the wall so that I could fasten it to a sturdy bollard. This line was extremely long and it lay safely on the bottom of the harbour until I was ready to winch it in tight. I tied other lines from *Lucia*'s bows to the large piles on the pontoon directly in front of her.

The marina was a hive of activity as people attended to their boats. Until three o'clock I worked really hard clearing the decks of anything likely to blow away or add to windage. I was offered a small area in one of the marina buildings to stow my sails and other large items. All the other loose things I brought below. My dinghy, being too large to stow anywhere, had to stay on deck and I tied it down as tightly as possible. The last job I did was to lash the wind generator blades securely to the supporting pole, to stop them rotating. During all this time there was hardly a breath of wind in the air. José was buzzing around the marina doing his best to check on all the yachts and seemed pleased with my efforts.

An hour later Erik and I went to Peter's Café for a 'wet', as Erik calls a drink. Much to my amazement the place was packed with people enjoying a pre-hurricane party. By now the sky was completely overcast, with the wind blowing hard. There were white horses skipping across the sea as far as the eye could see. Within forty-five minutes waves were crashing over the harbour wall and the noise of the wind had grown quite alarming.

Although I had always promised Paul that if possible I would stay ashore in such conditions, now that the situation had arisen I felt unable to abandon *Lucia*. I had to be on board to do whatever I could to protect her. I struggled to keep my footing on the pontoon as I fought my way back to her against the driving wind and rain. If I had left Peter's Café even fifteen minutes later it is unlikely I would have got safely back aboard.

Before I went below I checked my lines to make sure the rubber hoses were still in place to prevent the lines from chafe. With the cockpit door firmly closed I sat on my companionway step, staring out across the harbour towards the sea. A few minutes later I watched with relief as Erik climbed aboard *Windweaver*. It was a comfort to know he was there. Looking across to *Montana*, I could see Ron on deck and hoped he would soon go below to keep his mother company. Diana, a remarkably brave lady in her late seventies, had confessed to me earlier in the day that she was very apprehensive of what was to come. I watched in awe as the waves crashed over the thirty-foot-high harbour wall and the raging wind drove the spray and rain horizontally across the marina.

By now *Lucia* was heeling at an alarming angle. I carefully stepped out into the cockpit to check on the stern line, which I was pleased to find was bar-taut. A sudden fierce gust thrust *Lucia* further over, knocking me off balance. I grabbed the handrail on the binnacle and pulled myself to my feet. Looking up, I could see that the wind generator had broken loose of its bindings and was rotating at incredible speed. I stared at it, wondering how I could get close enough to relash it without risking serious injury, but quickly realised this would not be possible and decided to leave well alone.

A movement on the pontoon caught my eye; it was Erik, struggling to attach another line from *Windweaver* to the dock. As I turned into the wind to look at him the pressure on my face felt as if I was riding on a motorbike at a hundred miles an hour. The salt spray was blinding, so hanging on to the line on my winch, I ducked down into the cockpit. Erik was pointing at my generator, shouting something, but although he was only ten feet away I could not hear a single word. I shook my head and made signs to tell him to stay clear of the generator. He nodded, pointed at me, then held his hand to the side of his face indicating we should talk on the radio.

As soon as I was below I switched on the regulator for the wind generator; this is a device for dumping power to prevent the batteries from blowing up. Within a few moments the regulator was too hot to touch. I called Erik on the radio and we agreed it would be lethal to attempt to restrain the generator.

The noise of the storm was dreadful. I wedged myself into my chair, played some music to try and drown out the ferocious wind noise and breathed deeply to calm myself. I jumped out of my skin as Erik's voice suddenly boomed over the radio. 'Mo, you must drop your stern line. There's somebody in an open boat heading straight for it.' I dashed into the cockpit and through the blinding spray I could just make out a small boat approaching astern of *Lucia*. I was terrified that the man on it would be swept overboard if he collided with the taut line. As I wrestled to try and release the line from the winch I saw the man's hand reach up, grab hold of it and use it to propel his boat forward and behind the lee of the large motor yacht the other side of *Lucia*. I crouched in the cockpit and waited with bated breath. After what seemed an age, to my relief I saw him stagger along the pontoon towards the marina buildings.

Back down below I contacted Erik, and we marvelled at the lucky escape this man had had. I sat in my companionway watching with trepidation as the storm gathered in strength. The most daunting aspect was not knowing what heights it would reach or how long it would last. It was almost 11p.m. when the hurricane began to abate; the drop in noise level was a great mercy. After a while Erik called me on the radio and suggested we go to Peter's Café.

'Are you sure it's safe to leave the boats?'

'Yes, it's over now and I'm in great need of a wet!'

There was not a light in sight, so with the aid of torches we stumbled in the direction of the café. There was debris strewn everywhere – huge branches, complete trees, even concrete lamp-posts. We stepped carefully to avoid bare electrical cables and telegraph poles that had been dashed to the ground.

Erik was out of luck: Peter's was closed and boarded up, as were many other buildings we passed. On our way back to the marina I noticed that the wind had completely died. Suddenly a dreadful thought entered my mind.

'Erik, you don't think this could be the eye of the hurricane, do you? I mean, any moment now we could get hit from the opposite direction?'

'You know, that's just what I was thinking.'

We rushed back to our boats and within minutes, as we had suspected, the wind blew from the opposite direction and was once more screaming in the rigging. The storm raged for a further three hours. When it was finally over I was completely drained and fell into an exhausted sleep.

Some hours later I awoke and tried to get up, but my whole body screamed at me. Feeling as stiff as a board, I moved around very slowly for a while and did some gentle exercises to ease my strained muscles. Out on deck, I examined *Lucia* to assess any damage that had occurred. With relief I noted that she had fared very well – even the wind generator had survived its jet-propelled action. I lowered the rope on the winch so that it could sit on the bottom of the harbour, out of harm's way, until I could undo it from the bollard and pull it back aboard. Ron from *Montana* was on the wall adjusting his lines, so I called over to him.

'Any damage, Ron?'

'Nothing. How about you?'

I gave him the thumbs-up sign and promised to call round and see Diana a little later.

I glanced up at the hills overlooking the harbour and was really sad to see the picturesque old flour mill devoid of its roof and sails. It looked like a lone broken tooth sticking up in the gum of the earth. Erik soon appeared looking just as I felt, hurricane-battered. *Windweaver*, like *Lucia*, had survived unscathed. He was unable to contact Daphne, who had stayed in their friend's house, because all the telephone lines were down, so he hurriedly made his way there. He promised they would both return later so that I could see for myself that Daphne was all right.

The island was without electricity and telephones for over ten days – in fact some remote areas were not back to normal for several weeks. The beauty of living aboard was that I had no need of these land-based facilities; in fact life for me got back to normal very quickly. The one problem I did suffer was what I can only describe as 'hurricane hangover'. My body felt as if all its muscles had been stretched to the limit and then suddenly released. It was later reported that Tania had produced winds of up to 120 miles an hour in the harbour. This was definitely one experience I was not in a rush to repeat!

CHAPTER TWELVE

BRASS TACKS

The remaining winter months passed without further extremes of weather, to my relief. We did experience strong winds for long periods of time, but nothing to compare with Hurricane Tania.

For Christmas and New Year I decorated *Lucia* in very traditional fashion, including a real tree. Paul flew out for another month's holiday, which made the festive season really special. Daphne and I combined forces to produced a proper Christmas dinner. We managed to buy a turkey – not an easy item to come by in Horta – whom we named Umberto after a rather chubby, jovial man who lived on the island. The weather on Christmas Day was absolutely beautiful. Erik, Daphne and their niece Irma arrived in the morning, bearing the perfectly cooked Umberto. He had been far too big to cook in *Lucia*'s little oven, so Daphne had done the deed on the stove in the house they were still looking after. Then we all trooped over to Peter's Café, where we met up with a host of other people to enjoy pre-lunch drinks and telephone calls to our families back home. Back on *Lucia* we sat in the cockpit, dressed in shorts and T-shirts, and soaked up the sunshine until we retired below to indulge in hours of eating, drinking and laughter.

New Year's Eve was magical. Paul and I were joined by a group of friends on *Lucia*, then we all went from yacht to yacht enjoying food, drink and good company. At midnight, having worked our way around the marina, Paul and I arrived at the huge American luxury motor yacht *The Virginian*. The captain, who had earlier invited Paul and me for drinks, looked at me in bewilderment when I handed him a piece of coal. I suggested he show it to his chief engineer. He disappeared, returning at the heels of a giant Scotsman whose eyes were filled with tears.

'Skipper, do you realise what she's done?' he said with emotion. 'She's ensured us and the ship have good luck for the rest of the year!'

The captain, still completely at a loss, watched this burly man take me in his arms and hug me as he thanked me from the bottom of his heart for making his day.

Paul and I sipped champagne on the deck as we watched a splendid firework display in the outer harbour. Before we took our leave the captain handed us each his card and made us promise to visit him if we were ever in Fort Lauderdale, Florida.

Before Paul returned to England, I was delighted to learn that he planned to sail *Faiz III* to Horta in late spring. Then we hoped to cruise in convoy to many of the Azores islands before sailing further afield. In the meantime, once again we had to endure a tearful farewell and the heartbreak of a long separation.

My idyllic lifestyle in Horta was briefly marred by one incident. I had been enjoying a very pleasant evening in Peter's Café with a young English couple who were setting sail as crew the following morning on a voyage to Holland. They came back to *Lucia* with me to borrow

my alarm clock. After waving them goodnight I went
below, leaving the door ajar because the evening was so
warm. Without switching on the lights or drawing the
blinds in the saloon, I went forward to my cabin. With
these curtains closed, I undressed and slipped into bed.
A few minutes later, in need of a glass of water, I
walked through to the galley, had a drink and returned
to my bed.

But before I had had a chance to snuggle down there
was a knock on the hull. Convinced it was my friends,
maybe in need of another last-minute favour, I put on
my robe and went out into the cockpit. There on the
pontoon stood the marina security guard with his cap in
his hand, pointing at my windows and mumbling something I could not understand. I stood on the side deck
looking at where he had pointed and, seeing nothing
amiss, asked him to repeat slowly what he had said.

'I have been watching you through your window. You
have a beautiful body. I would like to come on and——'

By now, he had placed one foot on the toe rail. Before
he could come any closer or finish his sentence I raised
my hand to him and yelled at him that he jolly well
could not come aboard but must go away immediately.

I rushed below, locking the door behind me, then
quickly pulled the forward hatch shut and locked it.
Having drawn the curtains over the remaining windows,
I sat down shaking with fear. I tried to keep calm,
telling myself that I had managed to send him away
with a flea in his ear, when I heard another knock on
the hull. I held my breath as I felt *Lucia* heel when the
guard hoisted himself aboard. I listened in terror, to his
footsteps making their way along the side decks and into
the cockpit. He walked slowly around the deck before
jumping down on to the pontoon. Another knock on the
hull.

'I'm sorry to disturb your evening, OK?'

Without uttering a sound my mind screamed: 'No, *it is not OK.*'

Being the only live-aboard in that part of the marina, even if I had yelled at the top of my voice it was unlikely that anyone would have heard me. Although common sense told me he could not get in, I was still extremely frightened and passed a very worrying night. The next morning I reported the incident to the marina manager, explaining how afraid I had felt and that, although I did not want to make too much fuss, I also did not want the guard to feel he was welcome in any way. I was relieved when José told me later that the guard had been taken to task and, under threat of dismissal and police action, was forbidden to come anywhere near me.

Marijke, however, thought the guard sounded very polite and Helen, an American friend, asked if I would display a placard directing all would-be rapists to her address. Joking aside, this episode had had a profound effect on me and from then on I was extremely careful to lock my door and pull all my curtains. In hindsight I was able to see the funny side of this incident, but due to my life experiences old habits die hard.

In early March, coming back from a visit inland with Erik and Daphne, I received a message from Peter's Café that my sister needed me to contact her urgently. I was very distressed to learn that my father was dangerously ill in hospital. I arranged to take the first available flight to England and my friends rallied round to send me on my way, promising that they would take good care of *Lucia* during my absence. When I arrived at my parents' house, I was delighted to learn that my father was now on the road to recovery. Having been a very fit racing cyclist since he was a teenager, at the age of seventy-five he was determined not to hang up his bicycle clips just yet.

Soon after my arrival in England, Paul told me that he had arranged for us both to attend the Slocum Society's annual dinner in London. Then he asked me what I wanted to hear first; the good or the bad news. I opted for the good.

'We've been invited as guests, so the meal will be free.'

'Great! OK, hit me with the bad news.'

'You're giving the after-dinner speech.'

'*Oh, no, I'm not.*'

'Too late, Mo. I've already accepted on your behalf.'

'Well, you can just un-accept, Paul. I've never given a speech in my life and I'm not going to start now.'

'Trust me. I know you can do it – you'll be fine.'

During the two weeks before the dinner I often sank into fits of silent panic. No matter how hard I tried I just could not form the speech in my mind. I began making notes – pages of them. Eventually I whittled them down and kept going over and over the words in my head. But I would get so far and then not be able to think straight. I kept hoping something would occur to prevent me from attending.

On the morning of the due day, Paul brought me a cup of tea in bed. The first words I uttered to him were, 'I'm sorry, Paul, I just can't do it. I'm not going.'

'Oh yes you are, I promise you it will be all right. You'll enjoy it once you get there.'

During the long drive from Paul's brother's house in Bracknel to London Paul suggested that, when I was ready, I should look at the clock on the dashboard and start talking out loud. If I went right through to the end of what I planned to say I would have some idea of how long the speech would last. I got through a full thirty seconds before I became completely tongue-tied – apart, that is, from profanities!

As soon as we arrived at the Russell Hotel, I headed

for the loo. It was then, realising there was no escape, that I resolved just to get on with it and give it my best shot. The yacht designer Bruce Roberts in his role as Chairman of The Society and his wife Gwenda introduced me to many of the other guests, including David Sinnett-Jones whose yacht had sunk off Ireland during my voyage to the Azores. It was such a joy to meet David at last; we got on extremely well, and I greatly appreciated his wonderful sense of humour.

I have no idea what I ate during the meal, although Paul assured me it was excellent. When the moment arrived and Bruce had concluded his introduction I stood up and looked down at my notes, but the words just swam beneath my eyes. I pushed the paper to one side, took a deep breath, looked up and slowly began to speak. Soon the words were flowing freely from my lips. I finished by proposing a toast to the great master mariner Joshua Slocum, and sat down to very warm applause.

Before I had a chance to draw breath, David was standing beside me, offering his congratulations on my speech. He asked me to stand up and hold out my hand, into which he put several brass tacks.

'What do you think you should do with them, Mo?'

I was tempted to say I would scatter them on my deck, which is what Joshua did to repel pirates. Instead, I said, 'I don't know, David. What do *you* think I should do with them?'

Then he presented me with a brass plaque announcing that I was the 'Slocum Society's Yachtlady of the Year' saying, 'Use them to pin the award to *Lucia*'s bulkhead.'

I felt totally overwhelmed and my eyes filled with tears. I turned to Paul to borrow his handkerchief, and it was some moments before I had composed myself enough to be able to express my sincere gratitude to the members of the society.

LONE VOYAGER

I made a promise that I would endeavour to sail
Lucia to Newport, Rhode Island in June 1998 to attend
the celebrations to commemorate Joshua's completed
circumnavigation. David asked me if I could arrive on
time and not forty minutes early this time! When I
eventually sat down I was on cloud nine – and to think
that I nearly chickened out on this wonderful day.

My return to Faial was by an unexpected route;
instead of taking my seat on the plane, I crewed for Paul
aboard *Faiz III*. Paul also invited Philip to join us. We
had both been very upset about Philip's aborted trip to
the Azores and hoped that in a small way we could
make it up to him.

Back in Horta, I was delighted to be reunited with
Lucia. Now I had the best of both worlds – the
independence of being on my own yacht but with my
best friend, who just happened to be the man I loved, in
the same marina. Due to the prolonged nature of our
voyage Philip was only able to spend a few days on
Faial, but we did our best to make it a memorable time.
He and Paul rediscovered the paintings they had each
left some years before on the harbour walls, when they
had made voyages to Horta on their individual yachts.
Paul decided to renovate his artwork, but Philip chose to
let his continue to fade in the sun and salt air.

Erik and Daphne had moved back aboard
Windweaver from their friend's house and were hoping
to cruise in convoy with *Lucia* and *Faiz III*, though they
had a great deal of work to do before their yacht would
be ready. And with Horta's celebrated *Semar de Mar*
fast approaching, Paul and I decided to delay our departure. Paul entered *Faiz III* in several of the races, and
for two of them Erik, Daphne and I crewed for him. A
British couple, Alan and Leslie, who were sailing in a
yacht sporting an excellent figurehead of a brightly
coloured parrot, became great rivals with *Faiz III*. *The*

Parrot was one ahead in the racing stakes, and Paul was determined to get even during the last race of the week.

Faiz III and *The Parrot* were neck and neck for the first part of the race, and then on the middle leg *The Parrot* pulled ahead by some considerable distance. It looked as if we were destined to lose when, on the last leg, we were running down wind. Erik was at the helm, while Paul and I were raising every bit of sail *Faiz III* possessed. With the crew of *The Parrot* yacht yelling good-natured abuse at us, we gradually inched level with them. There was an enormous cliff face about a hundred yards past the finish line, which unnerved all the crew of *Faiz III* with the exception of Paul. As we crossed the finish line two boat-lengths ahead of *The Parrot*, Paul and I scrambled to drop the excessive amount of sail. To everyone's immense relief Erik managed to turn *Faiz III* away from the cliff in time, and we sailed back towards *The Parrot*. As we came level with them, Erik and Paul expressed their delight at winning by dropping their shorts and mooning at the losing yacht's crew! The excellent party that evening left both crews suffering hangovers from hell. I for one decided to drink nothing but mineral water for several weeks afterwards.

By the beginning of September, Paul and I were anxious to set sail. *Windweaver* was still not ready, but Erik and Daphne were confident they would soon be fit to go to sea and catch us up. With Daphne's help I left my modest painting on the harbour wall and then set about the marathon task of saying farewell to my many friends on the island. Feeling very emotional as the day of departure dawned, I took a last look around the marina and wondered if I would ever return.

Daphne and I were totally awash as we gave each other a last hug. With Erik and Daphne's assistance I slipped my lines and motored out of the marina. One moment I was waving to my friends, the next I was in the outer harbour struggling to raise my mainsail. Before I had time to point *Lucia* fully into the wind, the main halyard had whipped itself the wrong side of the mast steps. Eventually I managed to rock *Lucia* violently enough to flip the halyard to the correct side and at last raise the sail. *Faiz III* was by now quite a way ahead of *Lucia*, and when I was eventually able to respond to Paul's calls on the VHF radio we agreed that it was not quite the best way for me to begin my voyage.

We had earlier agreed to sail past Pico and Sao Jorge and head for the island of Terceira, where we planned to spend a few days before going south. I soon settled down to the joys of sailing single-handed, and as I watched *Faiz III* in the distance I hoped Paul was feeling the same. He called me frequently on the VHF radio, and at first I thought he was doing so for my benefit. As the day drew to a close I suggested we leave it longer between calls, but I could sense Paul's reluctance. Although I did not say so, I felt Paul might not be deriving the same amount of pleasure as I was from sailing alone.

Paul arrived at the peaceful harbour of Praia da Vitoria an hour ahead of me, at 10a.m. on the morning after leaving Horta. He called me to give me the good news that, instead of anchoring, we could berth alongside the newly constructed pontoon free of charge. As I made my way towards the pontoon, I was delighted to see that we were the only visiting yachts in the harbour. After we had checked in with the harbour master, Paul and I had a welcome meal together aboard *Lucia* before Paul retired to *Faiz III* so that we could each catch up on our night's lost sleep.

Over the next three days we had great fun exploring Terceira. The next island we stopped at was Sao Miguel; conditions were just right and we had an excellent sail. Once again, to Paul's great amusement, he arrived a few hours ahead of me. We met up with many of my old friends on the island and stayed six days instead of the planned three.

A few hours before nightfall we set sail for the last of the Azores islands on our route, Santa Maria. With a passage of just over fifty miles, leaving when we did would ensure making landfall during the hours of daylight. When we were a few miles into our voyage, a pod of dolphins surrounded our yachts. Once again I was delighted at the antics of these fascinating creatures. As darkness fell I watched *Faiz III* race ahead of me until I could only just make out the light at the top of Paul's mast.

Although this was a short trip I found it quite tough and felt a little the worse for wear as I approached the harbour of Vila do Porto. Paul had called me several times once he had dropped his anchor, advising me to make haste as it looked as if a change in the weather was imminent. Since leaving Horta I had not experienced a hint of seasickness, but I felt it was now about to rear its ugly head again. I battled hard to push these thoughts out of my mind as I prepared *Lucia*'s ground tackle. Rounding the breakwater, I could clearly see *Faiz III* lying peacefully at anchor. My anchoring experience had been minimal, and I was a little nervous as I passed behind her, heading for a spot just to the left and in front of her.

Paul was standing on deck and I indicated to him where I planned to go. I pointed *Lucia* into the wind, without taking into consideration the fact that the wind was blowing quite hard, and then put her into reverse to halt her forward motion. As I walked to the bows to drop the hook, I could hear Paul shouting at me from the top of his voice.

'Not there, Mo. You're right on top of my anchor!'

As I turned to look at him I realised *Lucia* was being

rapidly blown down on to *Faiz III*, and by now Paul was looking very anxious. I raced back to the cockpit and circled *Faiz III* once more, apologising as I went and promising Paul I would choose somewhere much further away from him this time. He began yelling instructions at me.

'Don't put her into reverse, and drop the bloody hook as quickly as possible.'

I picked my spot, rushed forward and just as I was carefully lowering the anchor I heard Paul shouting.

'Drop it! Just drop the——thing.'

I did as instructed and watched in horror as an enormous amount of chain rushed from the hawse pipe over the bows into the harbour. By the time I brought it to a halt I had dropped well over twenty metres in five metres of water. When I looked up, Paul was in his dinghy rowing like fury towards *Lucia*. Within a few minutes, he was on board.

'How much have you dropped?'

'Just over twenty metres.'

'Why?'

'Because you yelled at me!'

'OK, bring it all up and I'll show you how to do this right.'

By the time I had raised the anchor, repositioned *Lucia*, dropped the anchor and reset it under Paul's instructions, now calmly given, I was exhausted.

'Are you upset with me?' he asked gently.

'Yes.'

'I'm sorry, but I just couldn't believe you could get it so wrong.'

'Well, yelling at me didn't help one little bit.'

His arms were around me in seconds. 'I'm really sorry, Mo. I think we're both very tired. Do you think you'll remember how to do it next time?'

'Paul, rest assured this is one lesson that's now firmly

fixed in my mind.' I was ready for a fat argument until I saw a smile spread across his face.

'At least we've given anyone watching a good laugh,' he assured me.

We were sitting in the cockpit, chilling out with a cup of tea, when the pilot launch approached us. In broken English and sign language we were asked to move our yachts to a different position in the harbour, as they were bringing in a supply ship and were concerned that there would not be enough room to turn it around. Now I could see the funny side of this; Paul, on the other hand, could not! We moved *Lucia* in record speed, then rushed in Paul's dinghy to *Faiz III* and just about had time to drop her back a few metres when the ship sailed in.

The wind was blowing a real hoolie from the east by now, which set up a rolling motion in the harbour and made life aboard far from comfortable. Paul returned me to *Lucia* and we set up my 'flopper stopper'. This wonderful gadget that Paul had made consisted of a triangular piece of aluminium with a weight at one corner. It was hung by a three-legged bridle connected to a ten-foot length of rope. We suspended it a few feet below the water from the spinnaker pole attached to the mast, and its immediate effect was to reduce the roll. Although I had never used my 'flopper stopper' before, I instinctively knew this was one piece of equipment I could easily fall in love with. Very soon I had fallen into a deep, refreshing sleep.

After a few days of sightseeing we were faced with a dilemma: the wind was due to go south-east, which would render the harbour untenable, but it was also the direction of the next island we were heading for. Porto Santo lay forty miles north-east of Madeira and approximately 500 miles south-east of Santa Maria. If we left now, it would mean starting the passage sailing hard on the wind. This is always tough, but as it would be dangerous to stay in the harbour we were left with little option. We were also sad to leave before *Windweaver* had managed to catch up with us. Having no way of knowing where Erik and Daphne were, the only thing we could do was leave a message for them with the port authorities.

By late afternoon of our fourth day in Santa Maria I was hard at work studying the charts and working out my passage plan. This was going to be the first long journey I had embarked on for some time, and I was really looking forward to it. I also hoped it would give Paul a chance to get into the swing of sailing alone, so that maybe he would come to love it as much as I did. He joined me for supper aboard *Lucia* and we compared notes on our planned route, exchanging good-humoured banter regarding who would arrive first this time. I was in no doubt that *Faiz III*, being the faster vessel and skippered by Paul, the more experienced sailor, would arrive ahead of *Lucia*. However, my parting words were that I would have a cold beer waiting for him when he eventually arrived in Porto Santo!

Having slept really well, I was up bright and early the next morning to complete my pre-sail tasks. It is always important for me to feel confident that everything is stowed correctly. Items I will need during the voyage must be in order and close at hand, so that once I am under way my mind is free to concentrate on the sailing.

Because I was at anchor this departure was going to be slightly different from others, which made me a little anxious. Would it go without a hitch, or would I encounter just as many problems as I had on arrival? I knew how to do it in theory, and I had related the technique to Paul the previous evening. With a big smile spreading across his face, he confirmed that I did indeed understand how it should be done. However, putting theory into practice did not always go as smoothly for me as it should. As I tied the last restraining strap of my dinghy to the deck, I heard Paul calling to me.

'How's it going? Are you almost ready for the off?'

'I'm doing OK – should be ready in about fifteen minutes. How about you.'

'I've been ready for hours. Just doing what I'm good at – waiting for you.'

'Cheeky devil! Be off with you, man, you'll need all the head start you can get.'

I took one last look round the deck, then went below to visit the heads yet again. Then I tucked my hair beneath my cap, checked out below from the bows to the stern, stowed my picnic in the cockpit and started the engine.

With my heart thumping in my chest, I walked to the bows. Paul waved and gave me the thumbs-up sign as he gently motored past *Lucia*. Slowly I began to raise the anchor, making sure the chain didn't jam in the hawse pipe. As chain has the knack of piling up on itself, I paused every few minutes, bent down and put my hand through the hatch beside the windlass to push the excess clear. The windlass laboured a little as it pulled the anchor free from the mud. While I winched in the remaining few metres of chain my eyes were everywhere, looking anxiously around to see where the wind was blowing *Lucia*.

The anchor appeared, flipped itself into the correct position and locked in place on the bow roller as if by magic. Rushing back to the cockpit, I put the engine in gear, steered *Lucia* towards the harbour entrance, turned her into the wind and raised the mainsail. Then I put her on course, switched on the autopilot and went back to the bows to close the hatch, collect the winch handle and check on the anchor once more. After that I walked calmly back to the helm, feeling extremely grateful that this time everything had gone according to plan.

LONE VOYAGER

As I motor sailed away from the harbour I could see Paul standing on the stern of *Faiz III*, waving and gesturing for me to go towards him. I wondered what on earth could be wrong. Once I was within hailing distance he yelled, 'Smile!', pointed his camera at *Lucia* and began taking photographs. Then he directed me to alter course so he could get the best possible shots. Once the surprise photo session was over we wished each other good luck and a safe voyage, and then we were on our way.

The passage began with the wind coming from the east, and I enjoyed a few hours of good sailing in reasonably calm conditions until we had cleared the island. Then we were in the sort of seas that really slow *Lucia* down – short, sharp and choppy. My speed dropped below two knots and I watched *Faiz III* disappear into the distance. Before long I started the engine and motor sailed for several hours.

There was very little shipping about and I passed a pleasant enough night, even if we were being tossed around by the choppy sea. Not having much of an appetite myself, I was surprised that each time Paul contacted me he had either just eaten or he was just about to. There seemed to be nothing his stomach could not handle, from beans on toast to huge bags of toffees. Throughout the night, I could just see his masthead light glowing dimly against the sky. But as dawn broke, even with the aid of binoculars I was unable to spot him.

I spent most of the day relaxing in the cockpit and doing my best to munch my way through a few biscuits. It always amazes me how quickly time passes at sea, even when all I was doing between keeping watch was daydreaming. Before long it was time to tune in the radio for my noon sked with Paul. With the seas building and the wind hard on the nose, we just had time to compare notes and agree on the time for our next sked before I had to dash up into the cockpit and present the fish with the first of many meals they were to receive from me. As darkness descended, I nibbled on a dry cracker and wondered if Paul was still eating for England.

The next two days followed in similar fashion, and then the wind began to shift direction so quickly that the seas did not have time to catch up and the ocean resembled a boiling cauldron. During one of my short chats with Paul, I made the mistake of asking him how conditions were in his part of the Atlantic.

'Crap, utter crap. In fact complete and utter crap!'

'Oh, dear. Well, it won't last for ever, Paul. Do your best to keep your chin up.'

'Mo, how can you keep so cheerful? With your seasickness you must be having an even tougher time than me.'

'There you go – things could be worse. Now try and look on the bright side. I'll have to go now, Paul, it's time to feed the fish!'

That night as I lay in the cockpit it started to rain. I got up, had a good look around and then snuggled up under the hood, in the hope of keeping dry. In one respect I would have been better off going below, but I knew my stomach would rebel even more if I did. It was with relief that some hours later, when the rain eventually stopped, I stretched out along the cockpit seat. As I dozed between keeping watch, my mind wandered through a multitude of subjects.

I recalled the original plan Paul and I had made to meet in Lisbon, and the events that had led to our present pattern of cruising. I reflected how my confidence had grown in leaps and bounds since my arrival in the Azores. When Paul had suggested that I fly to England so soon after my arrival in Horta, I had been filled with dread. I had only just escaped from so many emotional problems back in the UK, and I needed time to strengthen my inner soul before returning, so that they could not invade my life again. I giggled a little as I recounted the incident with the skipper from the Spanish yacht. Then a strange feeling washed over me as I realised I had dealt with this bully in such a positive way. Maybe my healing process had been swifter than I thought.

A sudden noise like a dull thud brought me up short. I jumped up and looked all around, but nothing appeared to be wrong. I checked on Joshua, the wind vane self-steering, and he seemed fine. I puzzled over the strange sound for some time but could not come up with an explanation. At first light I put my head around the hood to welcome the day and there on the side deck was a dead squid – so that was the cause of the mystery thud. If his leap had been a little more athletic he would have landed plum in the middle of my lap. He would probably have survived, but I would have had a heart attack. I have a dreadful fear of spiders, and as I gazed at the dead squid he showed a remarkable likeness to a gigantic spider. Even though he was dead, it still took me several hours to pluck up enough courage to remove him from the side deck and drop him in the ocean.

Day five, and during my sked with Paul I was delighted to hear he had landfall. It would still be several hours before he made it into harbour, but it was a great relief to hear him sounding so much happier. He had a really good laugh when I related the story of the squid. Paul, like me, was still experiencing difficult conditions with frequent wind shifts and turbulent seas. This was one passage that we would both be glad to see the back of. I tried to be philosophical and find something about the passage to enjoy, but it was not easy. The sky had been overcast for most of the time, allowing just the occasional glimpse of stars at night and brief periods of sun during the day. Apart from my squid I had seen no marine life either, although I was spending most of the voyage in the cockpit which was an excellent vantage point.

The one thing that I did draw comfort from was that whenever Paul and I compared notes I had either just completed a manoeuvre he was about to tackle or the other way around. To have my sailing techniques occasionally mirrored by a man whose skills I greatly admired was very rewarding. However, my learning curve was still very steep and each time I went to sea conditions would differ. I was only too aware that I had barely scratched the surface of the knowledge I hoped to acquire.

Just before midnight I made contact with Paul, who was now very close to his goal. The bay at Porto Santo is huge and Paul was still not sure where he was going to anchor. If the harbour entrance was as easy as the pilot book depicted, he would go for it. If not, he would anchor in the bay until daylight. We agreed to leave the radio channel open so that he could contact me when he was settled. The next hour was a very worrying time for me. So many things can go wrong when you are closing the land and I was still a good fifteen hours away from Paul, unable to be of any assistance should the need arise. Just as my imagination went into overdrive – I heard Paul's voice booming over the radio, so I rushed below and snatched up the microphone.

'*Faiz III*, this is *Lucia*. Over.'

'Hi, how are you doing? Over?'

'Never mind about me – where are you? Over?'

'I'm safely anchored in the harbour. Mo, it's like a millpond in here. Over.'

'Oh, Paul, that's wonderful. Any problems?'

'Yes, I've just realised that I left my only bottle of whisky on *Lucia*. How long before you'll be in? Over?'

'You twit, that's not the sort of problem I meant! Over.'
'I know. It was a piece of cake, Mo. Nice clear entrance, plenty of room to drop the hook – yep, a real doddle. Over.'

We carried on talking for a good ten minutes. Paul's biggest problem now – apart from the fact that I had his whisky – was that he felt guilty that he was snug in a tranquil harbour while I was still battling away at sea. But I told him how delighted I was for him and that it was a great comfort to know he was safely in port. He wanted to call me in two hours, but I would not hear of it. I told him to get his head down and have a well-deserved sleep. We eventually agreed to a sked at 0900 hours, sent bucketloads of 88s to each other and signed off.

I wrapped my sleeping bag around me, gazed out into the black night and pictured Paul snuggling down into his warm, dry bunk, drifting off to sleep as *Faiz III* lay peacefully at anchor. It was a beautiful scene to contemplate in my mind as I passed what I hoped would be the last night of this turbulent voyage. As dawn broke I saw shearwaters skimming the waves in search of an early breakfast. I loved watching the skilful flight of these elegant seabirds and hoped I would see just a little more marine life before my trip was over. After plotting my position on the chart I estimated that at my present speed I should reach harbour by mid-afternoon. I scanned the horizon, but there was still no sign of land.

Although my appetite was still very poor, I forced myself to eat a light breakfast. It was important to boost my energy for the forthcoming rigours of preparing *Lucia* for harbour. My sked with Paul was most enjoyable; he had had an excellent night's sleep and was full of the joys of spring, singing the praises of his peaceful surroundings. He was also delighted to have spied *Montana* attached to a mooring buoy not far away, and planned to visit Ron and Diana later in the morning. I agreed to keep channel 67 open on my VHF radio so that Paul could call me at will, rather than at a predetermined time.

Down below I attempted to put things in order, but with sea conditions far from calm I soon abandoned this idea and returned to the cockpit. It was far more important to keep my breakfast in my stomach than to have a tidy cabin. With the aid of my binoculars I was able to make out a dark shape low down on the horizon, and a spark of excitement flashed through my body. It would not be long now before I too would be enjoying the delights of a peaceful harbour. I plotted my position on the chart – only twenty-five miles to go. Oh, how I was longing to have a shower and wash my hair. I studied the pilot book and hoped the entrance would indeed be as straightforward as it looked. Then I mentally went through the anchoring procedure until I was sure I had got it set in my mind.

Waiting for the island to come fully into view was a bit like waiting for a kettle to boil; it seemed to take forever. I got down from my seat on the stern, and lay full length in the cockpit and tried to sleep for twenty minutes. But rising excitement rendered this impossible and I had to force myself to stay where I was. Instead of sleeping, I daydreamed about my first meal in Porto Santo.

It was not until two hours later, when the clouds had dispersed and the sun appeared, that I could see the land with my naked eye. Back on my perch, I watched this dark, monochrome island take shape. The shearwaters were quite prolific now, and I found their antics engrossing. As we slipped behind the shadow of the land our pace slowed and I started the engine to keep our speed at four knots, then pushed it up to five knots. Why not? I had plenty of fuel and I was longing to get in.

LONE VOYAGER

As *Lucia* passed along the island, I was fascinated by its dramatic landscape. Porto Santo is a small island in the Madeiran archipelago. Its steep cliffs were different shades of grey and sandstone, without a hint of vegetation. It held its own special beauty, albeit a complete contrast to the lush green islands of the Azores. The sight of a solitary dolphin filled my heart with joy as he leaped out of the water very close to *Lucia*. Soon he was joined by several more, and I gave special thanks for being reminded that, no matter how tough the voyage, these moments of magic made it all worthwhile.

Paul's voice over the VHF interrupted my thoughts. He was anxious to know how close I was.

'It seems to be taking ages, Paul. I've still got just over twelve miles to go.'

'Well, get a move on It's almost time for a sundowner and you're the one with the whisky.'

I was surprised Paul had not been ashore to redress this situation, but he said he did not want to miss my arrival and that maybe his chronic thirst would spur me on.

'Paul, rest assured I will do all I can to put you out of your torment. Just promise me that, if as I drop my anchor you feel compelled to pass comment, you will do so under your breath. Otherwise I may decide to send your bottle of amber nectar for a swim.'

'I promise, I promise. Take care, Mo. And give me a call when you have the harbour mole in sight.'

During the next two hours I passed several fishing boats and was delighted when they responded as I waved. Then through my binoculars I scanned the magnificent golden sandy beach which stretched for three-and-a-half miles along the coast. As I resumed my search for the harbour entrance, an enormous ship came into view. At that same moment the VHF radio crackled into life.

'Mo, I don't know how close you are but be careful – the ferry is just leaving the harbour.'

'It's OK, Paul, I can clearly see him. Looks like I timed that just right. There's no way I'd like to be in his path.'

I went to the bows and gently lowered the anchor clear of the bobstay. Then I dropped the mainsail, tied it neatly and furled away the jib. It seemed strange not to have to get the lines and fenders ready. If I could only get this anchoring business right, it would make coming into port a lot easier.

As we rounded the mole I was delighted to see a flat, calm, spacious harbour spread before me. I slowly motored around and chose my spot, not too far away from *Faiz III* but not too close either, waving to Paul as I went. This time I walked calmly to the bows, even though my stomach was turning somersaults, lowered the anchor until it touched bottom and then paid out a little more chain. I waited until *Lucia* was lying to the wind, let out more chain to three times the depth, walked back to the helm and put her into reverse to bite the anchor in. Then it was back to the bows to pay out a few more metres of chain for luck, after which I found transit points on the land which I kept in sight until I was sure we were holding firm.

I was surprised to see Paul already in his dinghy rowing towards *Lucia*. When he stepped aboard he took me gently in his arms and whispered in my ear.

'You did that *perfectly*. Oh, Mo, it's so good to see you.'

CHAPTER THIRTEEN

TO THE CANARIES

Memories of my first night in Porto Santo will always have a special place in my heart. To be welcomed with such warmth and love from Paul filled me with joy. Having experienced the same conditions during our voyage, we shared an understanding that goes beyond words. From the conversations we had had during our time at sea, I was only too aware that Paul had not enjoyed his first long solo passage. I had to agree that we had not experienced ideal conditions, but all that was behind us now and I hoped the next trip would be completely different. As Paul handed me a cup of steaming hot tea, he told me that as soon as I was ready he was going to take me back to *Faiz III*, where he hoped I would enjoy the supper he had prepared for us. After that he would return me to *Lucia*, where I could sleep for as long as I wanted.

'Great! And I thought you'd just come over to collect your bottle of whisky.'

We spent seven wonderful weeks in Porto Santo – even though originally we had only planned to stay for one, we just could not drag ourselves away. During that time we put our bicycles to good use, exploring much of the island on them. Porto Santo is completely unspoilt by tourists and except for weekends, when local people frequent the beach, the great stretch of golden sand is almost deserted. With so few visiting yachts in the anchorage, those of us that were there soon became an extended family. I would often throw English tea parties aboard *Lucia* that continued well into the evening, when the liquid consumed would be of a stronger nature.

One day Paul was listening into the UK Maritime Net when he heard Russell, the American radio ham who had relayed so many messages between us during my first voyage. Russell, now sailing single-handed in his twenty-seven-foot yacht towards Porto Santo from England, had been enduring a dreadful passage with prolonged gale force winds. During the gale he had suffered considerable damage when a huge wave rolled his yacht so far over that the mast hit the water. Sailors refer to this as a knockdown. We had daily contact with him from then on, and did our best to keep his spirits up. As he got closer to Porto Santo I would relate to him the daily goings on in our small community. The night before his arrival I promised that, no matter what time he appeared, I would cook him a never-to-be-forgotten breakfast. The next morning I awoke to see Russell's battered yacht anchored very close to *Lucia*.

As soon as Russ came up on deck, Paul rowed over and brought him to *Lucia*. It was wonderful to meet this super man at last and be able to repay him in a small way for having been there when I needed his help. We had an instant rapport, and during the next few weeks the three of us spent many happy hours together. I was surprised when Russ told Paul that, during the worst moments of his voyage, he had got so low and mentally fatigued that he had seriously considered putting out a Mayday in the hope that a ship would come to his rescue and take him off his yacht. Then he remembered how I had endured dreadful storm conditions for days, and this memory gave him the strength to carry on.

With no modern facilities such as launderettes in Porto Santo, wash day was quite an experience. Paul and I would take our bundles of dirty washing to the pontoons in the marina, run the tap for a long time to clear the pipes of rust, and then begin the backbreaking labour of washing it all by hand. Strangely enough, we experienced great satisfaction when the job was completed. With the water now crystal-clear we would fill our gallon containers and ferry them back to our respective yachts to replenish our water tanks. Then we would enjoy lounging on board in the sunshine, watching the washing drying in the rigging. Life was so uncomplicated and stress-free, and I was happier than I ever imagined I could be.

Most mornings Paul would either carry out maintenance jobs on our yachts, write articles for sailing magazines or continue to work on the book he was writing about steel boat building. I would either help him or cycle into town to do the shopping. During our free time we would go for long rides or walks, visiting many interesting places on the island. The coastline is stunning and we found the arid land consisting of mainly sandstone and volcanic peaks fascinating.

Behind the 15th century church in the town, we came across the house where Columbus is reputed to have lived. It is now a museum and we marvelled at the skills of these heroic sailors, as we gazed at the ancient navigational tools on display.

The weeks slipped by quickly and by late November, although we were reluctant to leave, we felt compelled to move on to the Canary Islands. Paul's family were planning to fly out for a holiday, and he was anxious to find a suitable marina where he could welcome them aboard. Having enjoyed such an unspoilt island as Porto Santo, the thought of visiting one that was inundated with thousands of tourists was not something I was looking forward to. However, the Canaries were the next stop before setting off across the Atlantic, and *that* was something I certainly was looking forward to.

We set about preparing our yachts for the forthcoming 300-mile passage and waited for a favourable weather forecast. Out of the blue one day a postcard arrived from Erik and Daphne. We were delighted to hear that they had arrived in Santa Maria and in a short time would also set sail for the Canary Islands, where they hoped we would eventually meet again.

On the day of our departure conditions were perfect to take photos of *Faiz III*, which Paul needed for the articles and book he was writing. After saying a fond farewell to our friends, we spent an hour or so messing about outside the harbour to get what I hoped would be some excellent shots. Then we set a course towards the island of Gran Canaria. The wind had gone remarkably light and we both made only slow progress. *Faiz III* was a little way ahead of me when Paul contacted me on the VHF radio.

'How're you doing, Mo? Over.'

'Fine. I could do with a little more wind, but apart from that things are great. I'm really pleased to be out sailing again. Over.'

'I'm going to tune in for a weather forecast in about an hour, Mo. I'll give you a call on this frequency when I've got it. *Faiz III* out.'

While we were in Porto Santo, with the help of Ingrid on *Dando* Paul had set up his computer to receive weather faxes through his short-wave radio. This asset would prove to be extremely useful, even if we sometimes received forecasts contrary to our wishes. I was busy trying to gain as much speed as possible from the almost non-existent wind when I received Paul's call.

'Mo, the fax shows that our present conditions are going to continue for the next three days. I recommend we turn back. There's no way I'm going to take six days over a three hundred-mile voyage. Over.'

'Turn back? I've never turned back, Paul. I'll need to give this a bit of thought. Over.'

'You must decide for yourself, but I'm turning back. I'll call you in a little while. *Faiz III* out.'

I sat down, wondering what on earth to do – the last thing I wanted was to go back. I carried on in my forward direction for the next hour. Then I had the feeling that something wasn't right with *Faiz III*. Although I could see through my binoculars that Paul's yacht was facing towards me, he did not seem to be making any progress.

'*Faiz III*, this is *Lucia*. Over.'

'Hi, Mo. Over.'

'Paul, is everything OK? Over.'

'No, my oil pump's packed up. I've been trying to fix it, but so far I've not succeeded. Over.'

'OK, Paul. I'll continue to come towards you, and then if necessary I'll tow you into harbour. Over.'

'Thanks, Mo. I'd really appreciate that. *Faiz III* out.'

The decision had been taken out of my hands. We managed to limp back into harbour just before dark, and by then I had resigned myself to the situation. I just looked forward to setting off again as soon as the weather would allow.

Five days later, with a fair wind, we set sail bound once more for the small harbour of Puerto de las Nieves in Gran Canaria. The three-day voyage was fast, turbulent and incredibly cold. Within twenty-four hours I had lost contact with Paul and once again seasickness struck with a vengeance. But this time I made every effort to drive *Lucia* on, and there were moments of great exhilaration. No matter how ill I felt, I still derived pleasure from the power of the high seas and the speed of the clouds racing across the sky.

However, it was not long before the dreaded SS and the penetrating cold took its toll and I suffered periods of extreme fatigue. Due to the variable winds, Joshua had great difficulty keeping *Lucia* on course. Feeling too weak to stay at the helm for long periods of time, I used Charlie, my electric autopilot. For some reason I miscalculated the power that Charlie was using and soon depleted my batteries. It was while I was trying to contact Paul through the Maritime Net that the problem was brought to my attention. Bill, the net operator, was having great difficulty picking up my transmission and suggested my problem might be lack of power in the ship's batteries. I immediately started my engine to boost the power and was able to have a message relayed to Paul, arranging for a sked the following morning.

During my second night at sea I was unable to rest for more than a few moments at a time. With the wind over the quarter, it was driving the bitterly cold rain into every gap it could find in my foul weather gear. Each time I ventured down below to escape the cold wind, nausea overwhelmed me. I was forced to accept the lesser of the two evils and, with a hot water bottle tucked down the front of my dungarees, returned to the cockpit to endure the elements.

On the third and last night of the passage the lights of Gran Canaria were clearly visible on the horizon. Not wishing to arrive during the hours of darkness, I reduced sail to the minimum and slowed *Lucia* down. Paul, who was a few hours ahead of me, decided to press on. He too had been finding conditions most unpleasant and he was anxious to bring his journey to an end. Although the harbour we were heading towards was small, Paul assured me that it was brightly lit and he was going to go for it. With a promise that he would contact me when he was safely in, I tried not to worry.

I think it would have been easier to stop breathing. As the minutes turned into hours, my imagination ran riot as to what disaster had overtaken him. When his voice finally came through the airwaves, he sounded exhausted. Just as he had rounded the harbour wall the lights were turned off, plunging him into darkness. As he had inched his way forward, he had soon become aware that the harbour was full and there was no space to come alongside. He had then attempted to anchor in an area that the pilot book recommended. Unfortunately, since the book had been written there had been a landslide and Paul had been unlucky enough to have run aground on one of the enormous rocks lying just beneath the surface of the water. When he had eventually broken free he had tried to moor alongside a French yacht, but the skipper had objected strongly. Finally a local yachtsman had helped Paul tie up to a moored fishing boat.

When I entered harbour the following morning I was very concerned about the lack of space. Fortunately, Paul had obtained permission from the owner of the fishing vessel for *Lucia* to moor next to *Faiz III*. Feeling completely drained from my passage, I was determined to manoeuvre *Lucia* correctly the first time. She responded perfectly, and to Paul's delight I brought her alongside in a very proficient manner. He told me how concerned he had been about me when we were out of radio contact. I told him he had more than repaid the worry by deciding to enter the overcrowded port in the dark!

I was desperate to go below and sleep for a few hours, but unfortunately the port authorities were not happy with the positions of our yachts. They were very friendly and apologetic, but made it quite clear that we would have to move. As I looked around the congested harbour, my heart sank. I asked the harbour master if there was space for us in the small marina, but he shook his head. Then the skipper of one of the two yachts moored behind us announced that both of them would be leaving very soon, and it was agreed that we would move into those spots immediately they became vacant. All I had to do was keep awake for a little longer. Within a few minutes of our arrival the customs and immigration officers arrived and came aboard to clear us for entry. Once again they found it hard to accept that Paul and I were sailing single-handed, and went away scratching their heads in disbelief.

Maybe it was because I felt totally exhausted, but this time I did not feel my usual buzz of excitement on reaching port. It was certainly not a quiet and peaceful haven like Porto Santo, but it did have a distinctive charm of its own. Since it was a working harbour, fishing boats were coming and going at all hours. The breakwater had recently been extended to accommodate enormous ferry ships which would arrive at regular intervals between 8a.m. and 10p.m. After a few days I began to settle into my bustling new environment. I would watch in fascination as the ferries arrived and left. The captain's skill at manoeuvring these huge vessels in such a confined space never ceased to amaze me. The ship's bows would begin to open before they had docked, taking on the appearance of a giant monster about to swallow anything in its path. As *Lucia* and *Faiz III* were moored directly in front of the ferry berth, I often feared for their safety.

While in Puerto de las Nieves I was kept very busy. Somehow *Lucia* had became infested with minute black insects which were very reluctant to abandon ship. After disposing of a great deal of infested food I closed all the air vents and put on a face mask. Then, starting in the forward cabin, I sprayed vast quantities of insecticide into every nook and cranny. I closed each locker as I went, eventually backing out of the door and locking it behind me. I repeated the procedure each evening. In the morning I would return from my welcome haven as guest on *Faiz III* to hoover up the dead bodies. It was four days before the last of my unwelcome stowaways bit the dust. Each night as I stepped aboard *Faiz III* I would discard the overalls I was wearing and scrub myself almost red raw in Paul's shower until I felt clean again.

Although Paul and I would have liked to stay a little longer in Puerto de las Nieves, the harbour had no facilities for yachts – not even a tap to obtain water from. After nine days our tanks were running low and it became necessary to move on. We decided to head south to Mogan, and get settled in before our friends and families came to visit.

We had a leisurely sail down the west side of the island, and for the first time ever I arrived before Paul. As I came alongside the reception dock, tucking *Lucia* behind a small ferryboat, I was shocked to see hundreds of people milling about. I threw my lines to a man who offered to help and then hung fenders on my portside so that Paul could bring *Faiz III* alongside. The man who had helped me with my lines was a British guy called John, he and his crew member (also called John) had arrived in the marina a few weeks before and had been listening on the short-wave radio while Paul and I were sailing from Porto Santo. I asked them where all the people had come from.

'It's like this every day. It's a real tourist trap here.'

As I tried to digest this unpleasant information, Paul arrived. I was just helping him tie up alongside *Lucia* when we were approached by a marina official who requested us to go back out into the outer harbour and return in half an hour, when he would do his best to find us a berth. We objected strongly, but to no avail. With another ferryboat looming towards us we were left with little choice. The two Johns hopped aboard *Lucia* for the ride. I was glad of their company, as by now my mood was far from happy. Eventually we were allocated a berth and, after checking in with the authorities, Paul and I wandered around to assess the harbour that was to become our home for several months.

The climate in Mogan was wonderful, but the constant flow of tourists took a great deal of getting used to. There were, however, important reasons for making Gran Canaria my base for a few months. It was a very convenient location for family and friends to visit, and I needed to do some major work on *Lucia*. The most difficult tasks were to sandblast and repaint her hull. One of the first things I did was to check with the proprietor of the local chandlers that I could lift *Lucia* out of the water and carry out the necessary work in Mogan.

'No problem. Let me know when you're ready and I'll arrange everything for you.'

Unbeknown to me, this confident declaration was not entirely accurate.

Paul and I soon made friends with many of the other cruising folk, some of whom were just passing through on their way to Europe or to destinations across the Atlantic. Others were staying long-term with a dream that one day they would make the quantum leap. It was a bit like a warmer version of Falmouth Yacht Marina.

There was little opportunity to get to know local people, as most of Mogan was run by people from all over the world. Very few of them were Canarian, but those whom I did meet were very pleasant. My favourite meeting place in the marina was the Aloha Bar, which, although it was open to everyone, was like a second home to the British yachties. I always received a very warm welcome from its proprietors, Carol and Nick, and a party at the Aloha was certainly not to be missed. I enjoyed a very happy Christmas and New Year; the variety of fresh produce on the island was overwhelming compared to that on most of the islands I had visited. Paul and I indulged ourselves to the limit over the festive season, and the social life was quite exhausting. We had just about recovered when Erik and Daphne arrived in *Windweaver* – what a wonderful reunion we had. During the following few weeks our three yachts were moored close together and we never tired of each other's company. When the day of their departure came I was very upset, as I had no idea when our paths would cross again.

By now, Paul had confided in me that single-handed sailing was not for him. He had known right from his first passage alone and, although he tried to shake this knowledge off, he eventually had no choice but to accept it. He also wanted to return to England because he missed his family greatly. Unlike me, he was not ready to cast off for far-flung destinations. To begin with I was very sad about this decision, but we reached an understanding. After all, our relationship had survived long absences before and we both felt it was strong enough to continue to do so. He had never tried to clip my wings, and I certainly did not want to clip his.

In a quiet moment, I reflected on my own reasons as to why I loved sailing alone. It seemed that, no matter how dreadful the weather or how debilitating the sea-sickness, solo sailing held a special magic for me. Since leaving England, I had gained so much peace of mind and inner knowledge that nothing would deter me from carrying on.

There was, however, a sting in the tail of Paul's decision. He did not want to sail single-handed to England and asked me to crew for him.

'There'll be hundreds of people willing to crew for you, Paul, I protested.' Hardly a day goes by without someone knocking on our boats asking if we need crew.'

'I know, but I really would prefer you.'

Not wishing to return to England, even for a short period, I told Paul I would need time to think about his request.

The visits from our family and friends continued until well after Easter. Then we settled down to the important task of working on *Lucia* and planning Paul's return to the UK. Although I was reluctant to do so, I did eventually agree to crew for him.

'It will be just like a summer cruise,' he assured me.

'Well, if it's anything like the last summer cruise you promised me, I'm certainly an idiot to agree to go!'

The first time I crewed for Paul on *Faiz III* was on his voyage from Bideford to the Azores. He'd assured me it would be like a summer cruise during which I could relax and enjoy myself. As it was in June I had no reason to doubt his words. In actual fact we endured two horrendous storms!

When I asked the chandler to put the wheels in motion for *Lucia*'s refit, he was unable to live up to his earlier promise. I soon discovered that the word 'sandblasting' was like the kiss of death to boat yard owners. This is because it does make a dreadful mess as sand is forced along a hose under pressure to literally blast the old paint from the hull. I spent days travelling around the various yards pleading with people to allow me to carry out the work. Apart from a commercial yard in Las Palmas that would do the work for me and charge the same rate that they would for a huge ship, I drew a blank. Eventually Paul said we could do a temporary job by grinding off the worst patches, rubbing down the rest and repainting her.

'When you get to America, I'm sure you'll find a yard where the work can be done at a reasonable cost.'

I was very disappointed, but in the end I had no option.

All I had to do now was arrange for *Lucia* to be lifted out at Mogan – not an easy task. The local fishing co-operative owned the crane, and apparently it had broken down. However, I was assured it would soon be repaired. But there was no comparison between my understanding of 'soon' and theirs. After weeks of waiting I managed to arrange for *Lucia* to be lifted out at Puerto Rico, a yard further down the coast.

Paul and I would travel on the early morning bus to Puerto Rico to do as much as we could before the heat of the day began to slow us down. Then we would slog on until 6p.m. and take a much-needed shower before returning to Mogan. We would arrive at the Aloha Bar, eat our meal almost in silence, then return to *Faiz III* to rest our weary bodies. This gruelling task took eight days to complete, and we were one happy couple when we finally returned *Lucia* to her berth in Mogan.

Within a few days I left *Lucia* in the capable hands of my friends Hannis and Kate and embarked on the voyage to England aboard *Faiz III*. The passage, which took four weeks to complete via the Azores, was as far removed from a summer cruise as you could get. Having endured a violent storm just off the Continental Shelf, which lasted for several days, we had to run before the remaining strong winds into Falmouth. Here we stayed for four days, waiting for the next storm to pass. During this time, despite the torrential rain, Paul and I enjoyed visiting many old friends. It felt so strange being back in Falmouth again – a bit like stepping back in time. Nothing had changed.

But *I* had changed; I was now living my life to the full, no longer dreaming of what I wanted to do but actually achieving it. My desire to sail single-handed across the Atlantic was stronger than ever. I booked my flight back to Gran Canaria, anxious to return to the sunshine and *Lucia*. I had so much to organise before I set sail. Paul made our parting easier to bear by promising to visit me for a short time just before my planned departure date in late November. It was only when we were at Gatwick airport that the full realisation of our parting hit me. As the other passengers were boarding the plane, happy and excited about their imminent holiday, I was hiding my tears behind dark glasses.

Back in Mogan, to lighten my heavy heart I threw myself into the work on *Lucia*. During the cool of the early morning I would tackle painting the deck and then, as the temperature rose, I would carry out the work required below. Whenever I passed the spot on the pontoon where *Faiz III* had been, I would try to shake off my sadness with thoughts of sailing to the Caribbean.

Several new yachts had arrived during my absence. On my portside I had Peter and Sylvia from Britain on *Tradewind*. They were newcomers to the cruising life, and loving every minute of it. On my starboard side was Tom, a young Swedish guy who had been sailing most of his life and was now single-handing. I could not have wished for nicer neighbours. Like me, Sylvia and Peter were planning to head towards Grenada in the southern Caribbean, while Tom was heading to the northern part, to Antigua. The excitement and frantic activity on board our three vessels created great interest amongst the rest of the yachts on the pontoon.

My sister Valerie surprised me by flying out, with her partner Buff, to stay in a hotel a few miles down the coast from the marina. I took some time off work on *Lucia* to be with them, which did me a power of good. Unfortunately, Val was not convinced that my proposed trip was a good idea. I did my best to persuade her to look at it from my point of view, but I think I failed.

During one of my long telephone calls to Paul he asked me to draw up a list of jobs that would benefit from his skills; these he would complete in the first few days of his visit. Then we could enjoy the rest of his stay, knowing that *Lucia* was ready for the off. I had made a lot of lists since my return from England. No sooner had I crossed off one completed task than I added another two. I began to wonder if I would ever be ready.

A week before Paul was due to arrive I lowered my anchor to the pontoon and laid out all seventy metres of chain, checked it over and marked it off every ten metres. Then I switched on the electric anchor winch and pressed my foot on the deck button. Nothing happened. The motor was turning over, but the winch was not working. This was a big worry. I would need my anchor continually in the Caribbean, and I had not got a clue as to what the problem was. Tom had a listen and said he did not think it could be too serious as the motor was still working. I tried to winch the chain in by cranking the handle on the manual side of the winch, but it refused to budge. Peter helped me to feed the chain back into the locker by hand. When I spoke to Paul that night he told me not to fret as he was sure he could fix it. I added this task and one other that was causing me some concern to the bottom of Paul's list.

In the evenings I would assess the information I had gathered, from other, more experienced sailors in the marina, concerning anchorages to avoid and those not to be missed. Then, as I made mental plans, I would study the new charts and pilot book of the southern Caribbean I had purchased. The excitement was building once more, and I was really looking forward to the end of the preparations and the beginning of the voyage.

The day after Paul's arrival he studied the list I had compiled and said: 'What's this? Number seven, practise downwind sailing?'

'Ah, yes. Well, to be honest it's a point of sail I'm not at all familiar with. I know how to do it in theory, but I'd really appreciate a lesson if we get time.'

There were so many things to attend to that, out of the fourteen days Paul was with me, we managed only three days of relaxation. The anchor winch took days to repair. The internal bearings had completely seized. After much struggling Paul decided the job required desperate measures and placed the winch on the gas ring on my galley cooker. After some time, when the casing was really hot, the bearings were tapped out with ease. It was then a matter of dashing into Las Palmas to find an engineer who could make some new parts, while Paul and I went in search of new bearings before returning to *Lucia* and fitting the winch together again.

Another job that Paul thought would prove beneficial was to stick patches of sailcloth on the mainsail at the points where it was likely to chafe on the rigging. This caused great amusement amongst the other yachties, but any job that could save me problems at sea was well worth doing. Tom was in full agreement, and said being a single-hander was not something to take lightly. He was the first of us to set sail, followed a few days later by Sylvia and Peter. We gave them a great send-off. After that, each day hooters and people cheering would bring Paul and me on deck to wave goodbye to others setting off on the trip 'across the pond'.

Just before Paul returned to the UK we took *Lucia* out of the harbour to put her through her paces. When we were satisfied that all the repaired bits were working as they should, we set off along the coast so that I could try my hand at downwind sailing. Either as a result of my increasing tension about the forthcoming trip or because I was really nervous about using the spinnaker pole, to begin with I made a complete pig's ear of things. When at last I did get the hang of it I was exhausted, and on our return to the harbour I was violently sick. Paul found this extremely funny and I had to make him promise not to tell another soul!

The day before Paul's flight we drew up a list of radio frequencies and times when we would try to make contact. Once again, he promised to give reports of my progress to my family and friends. We had no idea when I would be out of range and I told him that when we lost contact I would do my best to give my position to the Trans-Atlantic Net, which with any luck would relay messages to him.

Our last night together in Mogan passed in a haze of mixed emotions. There is no easy way to say goodbye, even for people as practised as we were; in fact it just becomes harder. The next day, to help me take my mind off Paul's departure I resolved that once I had seen him off at the airport I would visit the supermarket armed with an enormous list of provisions. It took me hours to do my shopping. I had been warned that many of the Caribbean island shops would have limited stock and expensive to boot. So I had not only to shop for a passage that would take me between four and six weeks but also to lay in stores for many months to come.

When I returned to the marina in the hired car, it was full to bursting. I called in at the Aloha Bar to enlist the help of a few friends to transfer my purchases to *Lucia*. This was carried out with great hilarity. Alan, who was not a sailor, was totally baffled as to how one small woman could possibly need so much food. When the last box was loaded on board, there was hardly room to move. I returned to the bar to buy my friends a well-earned drink and ponder on the task of stowing all my goodies. In fact it took two days to pack my lockers and make detailed lists of what was stored where.

The final job was to plan my route, bearing in mind that I would have to remain flexible about landfall. The entry in my logbook read 'Gran Canaria towards Grenada'. However, with a journey of almost 3,000 miles ahead my final destination would depend on the latitude of the trade winds.

CHAPTER FOURTEEN

CHRISTMAS AT SEA

A plaque on *Lucia*'s bulkhead reads: 'A Journey of a Thousand Miles Begins with the First Step'. My journey of 3,000 miles began at 10a.m. on 2 December with a tremendous, heart-warming send-off. Horns were blasting from all corners of the marina and friends were crying, waving and cheering, as I manoeuvred *Lucia* away from the pontoon.

A German lady whom I had first met in La Coruna was running towards the end of the dock, frantically signalling to me to catch a gift that she was clutching in her hand. When it flew way over my head and plopped into the water on the far side of *Lucia* she looked very disappointed.

'Never mind. It will be an offering to Neptune. I'm sure it will bring me good luck,' I yelled at the top of my voice.

As I slipped out of the harbour towards the open sea, my heart gave a leap of joy and my trepidation of the last few weeks was replaced with a wonderful feeling of exhilaration! With positive energy I raised *Lucia*'s sails and set her on course towards a point deep in the

Atlantic, some 200 miles north of the Cape Verde Islands.

With very light, variable winds I made little progress during the first three days. So far, the only excitement I had had since leaving Gran Canaria was a large merchant vessel coming straight towards *Lucia*'s bows. It soon became obvious that they had not seen me and, although I was under sail, I had to start my engine and manoeuvre out of their way. Nothing is guaranteed to keep me awake on a passage more than a close encounter of that kind.

My total mileage for the second day was a meagre thirty. With the island of Tenerife still in sight I decided to motor sail south for a while in the hope of picking up a little wind. This worked like a dream, and by 6 December a front passed over us, giving twelve hours of strong winds which pushed *Lucia* along at a respectable five knots.

Early on the fourth day at sea I was resting down below when my sixth sense prompted me to take a look around. Through my binoculars I could see a catamaran motoring fast towards us. As it approached *Lucia* on her portside, I called the vessel on the VHF radio. The occupants – a German family, consisting of Klaus, Suzan and their sixteen-year-old son Felix – were heading towards the Caribbean too. They did not have a single sail raised and were wondering how I was managing to sail in such light winds. I explained that I was using a very light weather genoa and continually adjusting the sails to make the best of the available wind. After we had enjoyed a pleasant chat they motored a short distance from me and very soon raised their sails. I was pleased to see this, as one thing was sure; they could not possibly have enough fuel to motor the whole way!

The distance a radio signal will travel changes on a daily basis due to atmospheric conditions, known as propagation. So far this had been excellent and my daily contact with Paul was most enjoyable. It seemed strange that, while I was basking in the sunshine, Paul who was moored back in England, was keeping his fire going night and day in an effort to keep warm. Each morning on frequency 4417 a radio net operated among several other yachts who were crossing the Atlantic too. I found myself in daily contact with people whom I had never met, but as we were all of a like mind a strong bond was quickly formed. We were able to exchange all sorts of information and I was happy to pass on the comprehensive weather forecasts I was receiving from Paul.

During the next three days the wind, either from the north-east or the south-east, was up to force six, giving me my first real experience of downwind sailing. I struggled with the spinnaker pole each time I set the rig, but managed to complete the task successfully. After my first encounter with the argumentative pole I returned to the cockpit exhausted, and was soon hit by a bout of seasickness. No matter what the cost, it was certainly worth the results. *Lucia* was absolutely bombing along, covering record distances of 120, 140 and 130 miles respectively for the next three days. This was the fastest that she had ever sailed, and I was delighted with our progress.

Fortunately, before leaving the Canaries I had managed to obtain some Phenergan suppositories, and with the aid of this magic medication I soon had the dreaded SS under control. During these few days I also suffered from migraine and severe tummy pains, but eventually I recovered from all of these ailments.

For two consecutive mornings, due to sail changes or seasickness, I missed my check-in with the other yachts on 4417. When I did eventually call the American yacht *Sun Rise* Richard, the skipper, was pleased to hear from me. So was Wim, the captain of the Dutch yacht *Ala Queen*, who said he had been very anxious about me.

'I know there is nothing I can do to help you and I don't think it's of any use, but I just want you to know that there are a lot of people out here thinking about you.'

I assured Wim it was a *great* help to know that I was surrounded by the warmth and love of my fellow sailors.

One evening I called Paul at the usual time and he asked me to call back in one hour, urging me not to be late for the appointment. I waited eagerly, as I felt sure my son Russel was going to come on the air. I tuned in the radio full of anticipation.

'*Faiz III*, this is *Lucia*. Over.'

'Hi, Mum! It's great to hear your voice. How are you?'

To begin with I was overcome with emotion and asked Russ to do the talking.

'Paul's just been showing me where you are on the chart. It seems unreal talking to you like this when you're all alone in the middle of the ocean.'

'Russ, I can't tell you how wonderful it is to hear your voice, darling. You're coming through so loud and clear – it's as if you're here on the boat with me.'

Propagation was excellent and we talked for almost an hour, catching up on all the family news.

By now my life was beginning to settle into a regular pattern. Checking for chafe on the sails, sheets and halyards was part of my daily routine, as was clearing the decks of dead flying fish. I could have eaten the fish, but with seasickness waiting for any excuse to strike I felt it safer to return them to the sea, where some passing fish or bird would appreciate a good feed. I did my best to prepare light meals, which I always ate in the cockpit so that I could enjoy the view. As the huge, pewter-coloured waves tipped with white horses streaked towards me the sun shone through their peaks and they glowed a gorgeous transparent turquoise. I would sit for hours enjoying the sheer wonder of it all.

I was swiftly recovering from the effects of being in harbour too long. Now I had time to reflect and refresh my inner self. I had been looking forward for such a long time to this voyage, because I had been suffering from what I can only describe as an overdose of input from the human race. So far it was surpassing my wildest dreams.

Most days I would spend some time sitting in the bows, dangling my feet over the bowsprit, waiting for Neptune to kiss my toes with his waves. I was in this position one day, listening to the BBC World Service on my transistor radio and rejoicing in the fact that I had not seen another vessel for six days, when I spied the sails of a yacht coming up astern of me. I had stood up and begun to wander along the side decks towards the cockpit to find my binoculars when a whole shoal of flying fish leapt into the air close beside me.

I wondered what had spooked them. As I gazed, not more than three feet away from *Lucia* I saw a dark shape with a black dorsal fin showing just above the water. It was the biggest shark I had ever seen! I watched enthralled as he slipped silently by, and a shiver ran down my spine as I remembered that just a few moments ago I had had my toes almost touching the water. It certainly taught me a lesson – what if he had fancied a change of diet?

Through my binoculars I could clearly see a French flag flying from the stern of the approaching yacht. I called them on the VHF radio, but unfortunately the guy who responded spoke very little English. As I do not speak French, I could only understand a little of what he was saying. They were heading towards Guadeloupe. We wished each other good luck and they sailed on past.

Not wishing to return to the bows just yet, I sat in the cockpit and read for a while. I have always kept many books on *Lucia* and it was a real luxury to sit and read for hours on end, with no one to disturb me. All I had to do was cast my eyes around now and then to keep watch. If I got really involved with a book, I would often read by torchlight until the early hours of the morning. This was one such night, and at about 3 a.m. I spotted some lights in the distance ahead of me. At first I wondered if it was the French yacht, but as it got closer I could see many lights shining from it and assumed it must be a cruise liner. I could just make out its port light as it passed slowly in front of me some distance away.

This sighting confirmed my conviction that, although I would love to have gone below to sleep for eight hours at a time, as some people had suggested I should, it was not prudent. There is traffic crossing the Atlantic outside of the shipping lanes, and it only takes one ship to put you down. Sleeping between fifteen and twenty minutes at a time throughout the night might have deprived me of sleep, but it did afford me peace of mind.

I was feeling delighted at our excellent daily mileages of 120–130 miles and was slowly getting used to *Lucia*'s continued gentle rolling as we sailed with the wind behind us. Then one night the wind dropped to just a whisper. With very little forward propulsion, the huge ocean swell soon set *Lucia* rolling in an intolerable manner. I spent four hours setting the sails in a variety of positions, and eventually hit on a combination that gave the least roll. However, the motion was still extremely uncomfortable. I went below and wedged myself into my bunk, surrounding myself with pillows. Even in my pillowed nest, my body ached beyond belief, as I continually tensed my muscles to fight against the rolling motion of *Lucia*.

Thankfully, by mid-morning the next day the wind had increased and made up its mind which direction to come from. It took me over an hour to reset the sails, probably because my body was so tired and sore from a night of rolling and pitching. Finally satisfied that we were on course and making the best possible speed, I got as comfortable as I could and rested my tired and aching body for the remainder of the day.

Throughout my voyage, the GPS was not as reliable as I would have liked. From time to time it would bleep to tell me that there was 'poor GPS coverage'. Sometimes I would have no reading at all for many hours. Luckily, before leaving Gran Canaria I had brushed up on my astro navigation and, although I was annoyed with the GPS, I was confident that if necessary I could navigate without it. Joshua was working very hard during this downwind passage, and occasionally I had to give him a helping hand by adjusting the helm. Then the wind settled down from the north-east and for a few days we were able to sail along on the same tack. This was great, as it gave me a chance to regain some energy before the next 'battle of the pole'.

With a stable wind the sea became settled, and for the first time I was experiencing the immense ocean swell created by the trade wind. The waves appeared to be miles apart. I watched them approach from the horizon and felt sure they would peter out. Then all of a sudden, as *Lucia* sailed through the trough between the waves, I would be aware that I could not see so far as I had. The swell would lift *Lucia* up and gently let her down on the other side as the enormous wave passed beneath us. Although I estimated the waves to be at least twenty feet high, when down below I would be completely unaware of the swell. That's how gentle it was!

After thirteen days we had covered well over a third of the way, with approximately 1,800 miles to cover. A strong ocean current of up to one and a half knots was helping us along, and I estimated it would take a further thirteen to eighteen days to reach Grenada. It would be wonderful to make landfall and get a good night's sleep. Until then, my fear of being hit by another vessel continued to help me keep a good watch.

One of the most beneficial aspects of this long, lone voyage was the pure luxury of having time to think. Most of my adult life had been spent caring for other people, constantly concerned for their welfare and happiness and doing my best to solve their problems. Now there was just me to look after; at first this had made me feel very selfish, but my feelings of guilt were now slowly drifting away. At times I felt totally in tune with myself. Finding peace of mind had always been one of my aims in life, but until now I had had no way of knowing how uplifting and rewarding this would feel. I would often give thanks for this second chance; at last I was enjoying my life to the full.

We had a real red-letter day on 18 December. At 1515 hours GMT, *Lucia* and I passed the halfway mark. We were really sailing along fast and I wondered how to celebrate this momentous occasion. I thought I might do something outrageous, like have a glass of sherry, but as my tummy was not 100 per cent I decided to be sensible and wash my hair instead. However, because of the strong wind and boisterous sea I abandoned this idea too, as it might have resulted in an accident. I always bathed and washed my hair in the cockpit. This is great in calm conditions but with *Lucia* pitching and rolling I could easily slip on the wet, soapy floor. I would have to leave that pleasure for a calmer day. In the end, all I managed to do by way of a celebration was some cooking, a much safer pastime in such rough conditions.

I made a chicken risotto for the main course, followed by tinned peaches and condensed milk. As I then managed to get the contents down my throat instead of all over me, I felt I had done myself proud. Most of the afternoon I spent wedged into the cockpit, trying to keep comfortable as I read and daydreamed. Just before the sun went down I went forward and sat with a leg either side of the Samson post, holding on to the bar, riding the white horses of the Atlantic. It was a most exhilarating experience, but all too soon my bottom got really numb and I was forced to return to the relative comfort of the cockpit.

It had been an absolutely beautiful day, with temperatures well into the nineties Fahrenheit and a brisk trade wind to keep me cool. I recorded in my log that I had no complaints about the weather. Listening to the BBC World Service report on conditions in Britain, my heart went out to all my friends and family rushing around muffled from head to toe against the freezing weather as they tried to complete their last-minute Christmas shopping. And here I was, basking in the hot sunshine wearing only my hat and sunglasses!

How different this Christmas would be for me. I cast my mind back to the time when my sons were children. A glow of pleasure stirred deep within me as I remembered the wonder in their faces when I held my hand up the chimney to pass the letters they had written to Father Christmas into the safe hands of Tinkerbell. With a little help from me, they were convinced she would suddenly snatch the letters from my hand and disappear before we could even catch a glimpse of her. I could clearly hear their excited voices when, early on Christmas morning, they would discover that the empty pillowcases they had placed beneath the tree had been magically filled to the brim. *'He's been! He's been!'*

Christmas Day this year dawned with the most spectacular sunrise. I knew that a lot of my family and friends were concerned that I would feel lonely on this special day. But their fears were completely unfounded, for I did not suffer one moment of loneliness during this period or indeed throughout any of my voyages.

On Christmas Eve at 2200 hours the group that had been talking on 4417 got together over the air for a party! Richard on *Sun Rise* had organised it the day before and said we all had to do a turn. As I had already written a Christmas poem for my parents, I decided to read that and a quotation that I thought might give everybody something to giggle about. At the appointed time the yachts checked in with Richard and the fun began. I managed to record the radio party, and when I replayed it on Christmas Day it was so heart-warming it made me cry. Some people sang carols or songs with their own nautical words, others recited poems or gave dedication speeches, and some even played musical instruments. Words cannot describe the enjoyment we felt; for me it focused on the true mean-ing of Christmas. A strong feeling of love and good will was experienced by all.

One of the funniest moments came when a large flying fish leapt into Richard's cockpit. He thought it was his first present and planned to have it for Christmas dinner, but the fish had other ideas. When he attempted to bring it down below and put it in the galley, it slithered from his hands and slipped beneath the engine compart-ment, which Richard had left open to help keep the engine cool. He was unable to retrieve the fish until he got into harbour, which fortunately was only thirty hours later.

On Christmas morning I sat happily in the cockpit, opening the many cards and letters I had received before my departure. Part of my poem to my parents stated that 'I have no holly or ivy, I have no Christmas tree', but on opening my cards I saw that two of them bore beautiful pictures of Christmas trees. So *Lucia* was graced with more than her fair share on that day. I had also been given two presents before I left Gran Canaria. One was a silver-framed photograph of Kate and Hannis's daughter Lily. I was very fond of Lily and it was a joy to see her smiling face again. The other was a gorgeous teddy bear, dressed as a sailor, with the word 'Captain' embroidered across the front of his sweater. When Mike Warren gave me this present he told me that the one thing a single-hander lacked was someone to shout at. He hoped his present would redress that situation, but I could no more have shouted at this sweet creature than fly. I named him Captain Pepper after Mike's yacht, and he joined the happy band of soft toys on *Lucia*.

During the previous afternoon the wind shifted to east-south-east, so I had to change tack. This turned out to be a very difficult sail change, and as the battle of the pole got underway I felt my energy ebb. Lacking the strength to lift the pole over the guardrail, I sat down to rest. Suddenly the topping lift on the pole gave me a vicious smack across the face. It had the desired effect. With some very unladylike language I had that pole up and over the guardrail in seconds. I really thought I would have one hell of a black eye but fortunately, although it was very bloodshot, it did not develop into anything more.

Maybe it was the slight accident, or perhaps it was the excitement of the party, but after my sked with Paul at midnight on Christmas Eve I suffered a dreadful bout of seasickness. That night my sleep was interrupted by more than just keeping watch. Consequently on Christmas Day I felt unable to drink an alcoholic toast to my family and friends as promised. Instead, I made myself some tomato soup and toasted them all, one by one, with soup. Later in the day I did attempt to eat some tinned turkey and instant mashed potato, but gave up after a few mouthfuls.

By the time the sun had gone down I was feeling a

little better. Once again the night sky was spectacular, and as I sat gazing at the heavens I felt incredibly lucky to be experiencing such wonderful sights. Many of the stars and planets seemed to have their own subtle colour. As I followed the rise of Orion I felt very close to Paul, knowing that this constellation had a special meaning for him. During the building of *Lucia* Paul would relate many of his sailing experiences. He often described the joy he felt each night during his first long passages as he watched Orion travel the night sky. Last Christmas with him in Gran Canaria had been great fun. I remembered how delighted I had been when he gave me his presents – a Bowie knife and a large bottle of Chanel No. 5!

Then my mind skipped back to the last Christmas I had spent as a married woman. I had only been back with my husband for a few weeks after our first separation when Christmas was upon us. I remembered how I rushed around like a headless chicken, trying to ensure other people's happiness. Only Russel, bless his heart, guessed how desperate I was feeling.

I even remembered the red outfit I had worn. I had hoped it would give the appearance that I was in the Christmas spirit. However, my husband's critical comments soon dashed that prospect.

'A bit short, Mo. You're showing far too much leg.' Before we left for the hotel I went back upstairs and changed into something I thought he would approve of.

However, Russel's immediate comment of how nice he thought I looked in the red saved me. I changed back into my original ensemble. This time I did not have to respond to my husband's wishes. I wore what I really wanted to wear, *red!*

We were having lunch in a hotel with old family friends who had often been guests in our home at that time of the year.

When I took off my coat Alf said, 'It's Father Christmas in drag.'

'Mo, you look really lovely,' responded his wife Betty. A thought had flashed through my mind; why did I let my husband undermine my confidence?

I had been doing all right until, over dinner, one of them said how great it was to see us back together. The enormity of the sham suddenly became too much for me. I felt physically sick, made my excuses and went to sit in the loo until I had regained my composure. I wondered if these friends would understand, or indeed ever speak to me again when I finally left my husband for good!

Looking at myself now, what a difference I could see. With each day that passed my confidence was growing. More than ever now, I felt empowered to live as me and not as what others wanted me to be.

After I had plotted my position on 25 December, I calculated that I had about 544 miles to go. That meant, God willing, I would make landfall in four or five days. I was a little nervous about getting close to land again and wondered what problems I would encounter. But Pam, one of the ladies I had been talking to on 4417, gave me some useful information on Prickley Bay, the anchorage I was heading for, which encouraged me greatly.

By 2100 hours on 28 December I had only 120 miles to go. During my last radio sked with Paul propagation was very poor, and I was unable to make out what he was saying. The only way I knew he had received my position was when he responded in Morse. It was, nevertheless, incredible that we had managed to keep in touch across such a vast distance.

It had been a strange day: the wind had gone very light and the sea was really lumpy, making life rather uncomfortable. I did all I could to improve our speed, including motor sailing, but in such seas it did not help enough to make it worthwhile. When I eventually turned off the engine the peace was wonderful. I was sure there was going to be a change in the wind; all I could do was wait for it to make up its mind and then alter the rig accordingly.

As night approached I could see a faint glimmer in the sky, far away on my starboard side. I took a compass bearing, plotted it on the chart and was able to confirm that the glow was coming from the lights on the island of Barbados. It seemed strange to be so close to land after such a long time at sea. During the night, while reading my book in the cockpit, I turned off the torch and cast my eyes around. There on the horizon was the first ship I had seen for more days than I could remember.

The next day I saw a great many birds, yet another sign that land was not far away. By now the wind had changed direction and was blowing strongly from the east. This time I jibed *Lucia* without having too much of a struggle with the pole. After setting her on the correct course, I concentrated on calculating how many hours it would take to cover the remaining miles to Grenada.

It was imperative that I arrive during the hours of daylight, which meant that I must not allow our speed to rise above four knots. With the wind increasing, I was forced to slow *Lucia* down. As the evening progressed the wind became stronger and I reduced sail, reef by reef, until I was running under bare poles. I carefully monitored my position every half-hour, firstly because I wanted to know the distance I was covering, and secondly because my GPS was still unreliable, unable at times to give me a position for several hours.

When I spied the glow of lights from Grenada off my starboard bow, just where I thought they should be, an intense thrill ran through my body. If *Lucia*'s motion had not been so violent I would have leapt up and down

with joy. As it was, I was experiencing the worst conditions of the entire passage. I had placed a rope loop
around both port and starboard winches in the cockpit,
so that, depending on which side I sat during my rest
periods, I could slip my wrist through the rope to avoid
being hurled across the cockpit.

At 2200 hours my GPS bleeped at me, displaying the
message 'no GPS coverage'. All the waypoints I had
entered to guide me safely round the many dangerous
reefs lying in wait to catch a tired sailor out were no
longer accessible. I would just have to come into
harbour by the old methods. I was grateful that Philip
had taught me so well. Then, with just fifteen miles to
go, I was shocked when I felt nausea take hold of my
stomach. As I fed the fish once more, I despaired of ever
conquering this dreadful affliction.

In the dawn light I hoped I would spot the sea breaking over the most perilous of the reefs, the Porpoises. As
luck would have it, due to the very rough conditions
this was impossible as there were white horses everywhere. With all my senses on full alert, binoculars at the
ready and with every relevant chart and pilot book I
had on board to hand, I slowly made my way along the
coast until I was sure I could see the entrance to
Prickley Bay.

I felt I was being tested right to the very last when my
anchor chain stuck fast as I tried to lower the anchor
past the bobstay. I had to go below to the locker and
release the chain from the narrowest bit of wood it
could possible have jammed under. Feeling remarkably
calm, I returned to the bows and continued to position
the anchor ready for action. It took me some time to
decide where to drop the hook, as the white buoy marking the reef in the harbour was nowhere to be seen.
However, I eventually chose my spot and at 0755 local
time successfully dropped anchor. On 30 December,

after twenty-seven days at sea, I had completed my 3,000-mile voyage across the Atlantic. Once back in the cockpit I heard the familiar sound of my bleeping GPS, which was informing me that I had arrived! I almost launched it into the harbour for a swim.

CHAPTER FIFTEEN

PARADISE

After almost four weeks of swaying to the rolling motion of *Lucia*, when I first stood on dry land one of my legs felt considerably longer than the other. It took me some time to regain my equilibrium. While I sat outside the customs and immigration office, waiting to check in, I gazed out across the harbour. The sight of *Lucia* anchored in the beautiful bay, gently rocking as the clear aquamarine sea lapped against the palm tree-lined, white coral beach filled me with awe.

When I told the immigration officer the name of my yacht, a broad smile spread across his handsome face.

'Some friends of yours from the yacht *Trade Wind* were here yesterday, enquiring if you had arrived.'

I was delighted to discover that Sylvia and Peter, my neighbours from Gran Canaria, were still in Grenada. They were anchored in a bay just to the east of me.

After making several emotional telephone calls to my family and friends, during which I learnt the terrific news that Paul was planning to take the first available flight to Grenada I purchased a fresh loaf of bread and returned to *Lucia*. It had been so long since I had had fresh bread that the smell of it was driving me mad. I was sure I would devour the lot at one sitting, but after just a few mouthfuls I was full to bursting.

A few hours after my arrival I made contact with Sylvia and Peter over the VHF radio. Tears poured down my cheeks as they sang 'Congratulations' to me. Sylvia was longing to see me but was concerned that I should stay aboard and rest. But she understood that I was far too excited to sleep and we arranged to meet later that day. Our reunion was wonderful. Sylvia rushed to the dock, helped me ashore and hugged me until it hurt. Over glasses of wine and beer the three of us spent the afternoon laughing and crying as we recounted our voyages. They were longing to introduce me to all the friends they had made since their arrival, and as a huge party was taking place in the restaurant the following evening we agreed to meet to see the New Year in together. What a fantastic time we had – I danced barefoot until 2a.m., though where I got the energy from will always remain a mystery to me!

Grenada was just how I imagined paradise would be; a green, lush island fringed with white sandy beaches dotted with swaying palm trees. Hummingbirds hovered close to the most exotic flowers I had ever seen, and at night the sound of the minute tree frogs was magical.

When Paul arrived on 7 January my happiness was complete. We spent four marvellous weeks together, and made friends not just with other yachties but also with many of the local people. Two young Grenadians, Paul and Stumpy, really took us to their hearts and we were taken on a wonderful tour. With Paul, a very knowledge-able horticulturist, as our guide we hiked to the top of a mountain to see the rain forest. As we ascended he encouraged us not look behind by telling us we would turn into pillars of salt if we did so. He did not want us to see the view of valley and ocean until it was at its best, from the edge of the rain forest. Eventually we stopped and were allowed to look behind, and the incredible sight spread before us was so beautiful it made me cry. As I stood within the forest and looked up at the sun shining through the canopy of trees, my head swam with the incredible sight. The sounds of the insects and animals was intoxicating. I asked our guide if there were any poisonous snakes or wild animals that we should be wary of.

'Just the black scorpion,' he explained, 'and they are quite rare. A snake may want to share the warmth of a human body should it come across one sleeping, but there are no poisonous ones.'

He broke a vine trailing from a tree and let me taste the sweet liquid from it. Then he pointed out the abundant variety of berries, fruits and nuts. As a child the forest had been his playground and the only thing he carried with him when spending a day there was his kite! After exploring a little of the rain forest, we returned to Paul's home spellbound. Throughout the evening many of his relatives and friends dropped by to meet us, and Paul himself cooked us all a traditional Grenadian meal called 'Oil Down', an exotic dish consisting of layers of meat, fish and vegetables placed in a huge pot covered in oil squeezed from the pulp of several coconuts that had previously been soaked in water. When we returned to the harbour we were laden with gifts of colourful flowers, tropical fruit, vegetables and wine. My friendship with Paul and Stumpy will always remain dear to me.

After English Paul returned to the UK I spent many months in Grenada, enjoying my idyllic lifestyle. I continued to keep in touch, via the radio, with many of the people I had spoken to throughout my voyage. One day, while listening to the radio, I heard the familiar voice of Marijke, my friend from the Azores. She was now second-in-command on the *Aurora*, which was sailing in the Caribbean and was due to arrive in Grenada within a few days. It was wonderful to see Marijke again and to meet her new partner, Nan Dirk, and we had a great time catching up on all the events that had taken place since our last encounter. I was delighted to know that, like me, Marijke and Nan Dirk were soon going to head towards the north-east coast of America.

During my stay in Grenada, Rhiannon, my son Russel's partner, flew out for a holiday and we had a super time together. I was delighted to introduce her to the tough life of an old sea dog! I shall always be grateful to Rhiannon for persuading me to learn to scuba dive with her. Now I could not only enjoy the incredible pleasure of sailing on the ocean but also explore its bewitching hidden depths.

After Rhiannon returned home I prepared *Lucia* for her passage to Newport, Rhode Island, approximately a hundred miles east-north-east of New York. There was a sense of urgency attached to this voyage, as I had promised the Slocum Society that I would do my best to arrive in time for the centenary celebration on 27 June. The other aspect I had to keep in mind was the hurricane season, which normally starts in mid-June. However, this was the year of El Niño, which was throwing the world's weather systems into disarray. I felt a little uneasy that maybe a rogue hurricane might be lying in wait for me.

The day I set sail from Grenada I pushed all sad thoughts from my mind with the knowledge that one day I would return to this unforgettable island. Until then I would have no difficulty in recalling the sights and sounds of the magical anchorages of Prickley Bay, Secret Harbour and Hog Island, with their colourful varieties of bougainvillea and so many other exotic flowers; pungent smells of spices and the deafening sounds of the crickets and tree frogs at night. It was without a doubt the most awe-inspiring island to have made my first port of call after 'crossing the pond'.

My passage through the Caribbean was completely different from any other kind of sailing I had experienced. Voyages between the islands were not long, but they were far from easy. From the moment I left Grenada I had only six hours of good sailing. The rest of the time I was struggling against head winds and dealing with sudden squalls and thunderstorms while at the same time doing my best to avoid the vast number of vessels sailing in these busy waters. This type of sailing was far removed from the relative peace and ease of my passage across the Atlantic.

However, the time I spent on Union Island, Bequia and St Lucia was extremely rewarding.

On arrival in Union Island I had the unique pleasure of being the only yacht in the anchorage of Chatham Bay. The holding in parts of this beautiful bay is not good and it took me three attempts before *Lucia* was securely anchored. That evening as the sun went down, I sat on board watching the comic fishing antics of the numerous pelicans who nest in the bay. I blessed the day I decided to make sailing my way of life. The next evening I was taken ashore by one of the local people and enjoyed an excellent meal of barbecued lobster, cooked on the beach under the magical light of a full moon.

By the time I arrived at Prince Rupert Bay, Dominica, it was the middle of May. I made the decision, after spending a few days preparing *Lucia*, that I would leave the Caribbean and set out into the Atlantic to sail direct to Bermuda, a distance of some 1,100 miles. Then it would be straight on to Newport, Rhode Island.

I tried to relax for a few hours after arriving in Dominica, but from the moment I dropped anchor in the bay I had a nagging doubt as to how secure we actually were. To be on the safe side I stayed aboard for the rest of the day. Later that afternoon, although we showed no signs of dragging, I was unable to shake off my concern about the anchor. Before night fell I decided to put my newly acquired diving skills to good use.

Wearing my snorkelling kit, I am ashamed to say it took me twenty minutes to pluck up courage to make the dive. As I followed the chain down, I saw that it was wound around two huge rocks that were some distance apart. When I found the anchor I discovered it was lying on its side with no more than an inch of it dug into the ground. Looking to my left, I could see a clear patch of sand. On my way back to the surface I untangled the chain and then, climbing aboard *Lucia*, reset the anchor. Then I dived again to double check that all was well. This time I could clearly see that the anchor was well dug in. Now I would be able to leave *Lucia*, feeling confident that she would be there on my return.

The next morning I launched my dinghy and went ashore at the Coconut Beach Hotel. Landing the dinghy in the swell was quite hairy and brought knowing smiles from a few of the locals. Once I had regained my dignity I went in search of the hotel owners, who according to the pilot guide offered a special transport service for yacht crews. When I finally tracked them down, I discovered that nothing was too much trouble for them. They drove me into town, where my single-handed status created quite a stir as I checked in at the customs and immigration offices.

Back at the hotel, I could not help noticing how basic and run-down it was. Building work was going on close by. When I asked what was being built, I learnt that this part of the island had been hit very severely in the last hurricane and the owners of the Coconut Beach Hotel were now in the process of rebuilding. With the hurricane season fast approaching, I uttered a silent prayer that Dominica would escape unscathed this year.

While sailing from island to island, some other yachtspeople had told me that I must be very careful in Dominica. 'A woman alone', they warned me, could encounter some problems from the islanders. Fortunately this proved to be totally untrue, and I was treated with the utmost respect, kindness and affection. Soon after my arrival I was lucky enough to meet a young man called Chrispin Lewis. Early one morning, with Chrispin as guide, I took a canoe ride along Indian River in company with an American couple. We set off just after dawn. The mist rising from the river gave everything a dream-like quality. Huge land crabs scrambled across ancient tree roots edging the river. Large, exotic birds took flight as our canoe approached and unseen animals scampered through the undergrowth.

Although I should have left the island the next day, having seen the fantastic Indian River I felt I had to stay longer. Under Chrispin's expert guidance we hiked deep into the mountainous part of the island, emerging into a clearing where I stood speechless before a beautiful waterfall, beneath which lay the Emerald Pool. Within a few moments we were swimming in the cool water and, holding Chrispin's hand, I walked underneath the waterfall and experienced the incredible force of the cascade. After we felt completely refreshed, we drove around the rest of the island and I enjoyed many other wonderful sights including the Carib Indian Reserve. As we drove along the coast, I was amazed to see wild pineapples growing at the side of the road. This was yet another island to which I planned to return.

In the meantime, I had to make tracks. With increased urgency I filled *Lucia*'s water and fuel tanks, topped up my fresh food supplies and set sail for Bermuda. I had an exhilarating sail around the north of Dominica as I headed east towards the Atlantic. Due to the strong head wind I had to put in several long tacks, and it was not long before I got a rush of adrenaline as I left the Caribbean behind and sailed swiftly into the Atlantic!

I set *Lucia* on a course due north and settled down to life at sea. It felt terrific – *Lucia* gathered up her petticoats and we sailed really fast. Because we kept the east wind for many days, we achieved daily mileages of between 110 and 140. For the first four days my stomach was very unsettled, but this time I was sick only once. A thought crossed my mind that maybe at long last I was overcoming this dreadful affliction. As the days slipped by, I began to enjoy myself more and more. I passed my time doing maintenance jobs around *Lucia* and for the first time ever on a passage cooking fresh food and being able to eat it.

From my radio conversations with Marijke and Nan Dirk, well on their way to Newport, I learnt that the wonderful weather I was now experiencing would unfortunately soon be a dim memory. For the last few days of my voyage the wind completely disappeared and I was forced to motor sail, which was a little disappointing. Having enjoyed such excellent sailing at the outset, I had hoped to continue sailing for the full distance. The only other frustrating point was that propagation was very poor. Radio contact with Paul seemed to consist solely of my repeated messages so that he could just copy my position. The only reply I was able to understand was when he responded in Morse. On the lighter side I had the company of some beautiful black and white birds with long, swallow-type tails. I later discovered that these were the long-tail tropicbirds that signify the arrival of summer in Bermuda.

Although I had a good chart and pilot book for Bermuda, I was still a little anxious as I advanced towards the island. I plotted my position on the chart every hour, making sure I approached the island on its east side as reefs extended for many miles on all the other sides. I was fifteen miles south-east of Bermuda and there was still no sign of land. Two hours later I was beginning to doubt my navigation when, through my binoculars on my portside, I saw what looked like a breaking wave. I focused on this spot for several moments and, when I was sure it was not moving, I gave a yelp of delight. Land, *yes, yes, land*! Just six miles off, what at first I had thought was surf from a breaking wave materialised into the white rooftops of houses on the coast. Once more I experienced the exquisite thrill of landfall.

CHAPTER SIXTEEN

WELCOME TO AMERICA

A 650-mile voyage lay ahead of me to reach Newport and fulfil my promise to the Slocum Society. Although this promise sometimes weighed heavy on me, I could now see that if I did not dally too long in Bermuda I would indeed make it on time. With this fact in mind, I was able to relax and enjoy myself.

The day after my arrival I met a wonderful British couple, Rhona and Alan, who had been cruising for many years. They invited me to join them on board *Second Chance* for dinner and I spent an enjoyable evening getting to know these amazing people; both well into their seventies, they delighted in telling me that the cruising life certainly beat being in an old people's home. Shortly after *Lucia* three other yachts arrived bearing friends I had made in Falmouth and the Caribbean. I was especially relieved to see *Felicidade* and *Albert Conrad* as I had been talking to Debbie and Mort, the respective skippers of these yachts, on the radio while they were enduring a dreadful storm at sea. Even in St George's harbour we had had a rough time, with winds of over forty miles an hour. I was ashore the day the storm struck, patiently filling out forms for my visa at the US Consulate. After a risky trip in my dinghy I eventually got back to *Lucia* soaked to the skin. I was unable to leave her for the following two days.

Once the storm had abated, I returned to the Consulate to collect my visa. At last I had all the documents necessary to enter the USA. The final piece of the jigsaw was a good weather window in which to set sail. Unfortunately, that was not forthcoming. However, due to this delay I was able to enjoy my first evening of culture for some time when I attended an open air classical concert. During the interval I struck up conversation with the family sitting next to me and was delighted to accept an invitation to dinner the following day. One of the questions they asked me during my visit to their home was what I missed most about living on a boat instead of a house. This was an easy one to answer.

'Lounging in a bath,' I exclaimed.

Without hesitation these super people insisted that I indulge myself in this long-forgotten pleasure.

Two days later I was still waiting for the right weather conditions. While I had been in Bermuda the weather had either been dead calm or blowing a gale. I wanted to arrive in Newport with a few days in hand to recuperate before the celebrations, but at this rate I would be hard pushed even to arrive there on time. I consulted with Paul, who advised me that the recent weather pattern suggested it would be better to leave sooner rather than later. I found it unnerving to set sail without a favourable weather forecast, but on the plus side it looked as if anything bad was going to come from behind. Running before bad weather is a whole lot easier that trying to sail into it. Paul also gave me the wonderful news that he would do his best to get a flight to Newport in time to meet me.

On 10 June I hauled anchor and topped up my fuel

and water tanks. Then I passed through the anchorage, waving goodbye to my friends, and made a graceful exit through the narrow passage known as the Town Cut. I had to sail a good way east to avoid the reefs before setting *Lucia* on a northerly course for America. Within a few hours the wind had died and *Lucia* and I were motor sailing into a very choppy sea. Somewhere further north, I deduced, there must be some bad weather. I hoped with all my heart that it would dissipate before I reached its latitude.

Before the end of the day seasickness returned with a vengeance. With the strong possibility of other shipping in my vicinity I felt it would be imprudent to use the Phenergan medication as it was apt to make me drowsy. I was left with no choice but to endure the dreadful SS – and to think that on my previous passage I thought I had overcome this problem!

I checked in with Herb, a dedicated radio ham who operates a net on the short-wave radio, at 2000 hours GMT. Herb gives accurate weather information to yachtspeople, and as his net is extremely busy you need to log in twenty minutes beforehand, giving your name and position. After logging in at the appointed time I returned to the radio and waited to see if I was lucky enough to be on his list. Not only was I on the list but, because of my position, Herb had put me just a few yachts down from the top. I had listened to his net during my trans-atlantic passage, but this was the first time I had made direct contact with him. As my voyage progressed, I was to find his help invaluable.

Conditions were very uncomfortable and frustrating for the first few days. Being bluff-bowed, *Lucia* would come to a virtual stop as the steep seas hit her, knocking the light wind out of her sails. Then the wind picked up from the south-west and we began to sail really well. Unfortunately, the wind continued to pick up and we had a gale to contend with for the next two days. The only good thing about this gale was, as I had expected, that it was from behind.

The seas built up to incredible heights, and in no time at all we were running in heavy rain with just a storm jib raised. When I was convinced there was nothing further I could do to ensure our safety I went below, got as comfortable as I could and set my alarm every fifteen minutes to keep checking on our progress. I tried to comfort myself with the knowledge that it would not last forever, but my stomach was not convinced and sea-sickness once more became my worst enemy. When the worst of the gale was over I was gratefully relieved – until, that is, I learnt from Herb that I was entering an area of severe thunderstorms.

As I watched the disco lights of lightning dancing on the horizon my thoughts were of Joshua Slocum, who had endured similar weather conditions during his voyage to Newport. At this moment in time I felt extremely close to him. Was history repeating itself once more? I recalled a particular passage from his book;

> 'On this day there was soon wind enough and to spare. The same might be said of the sea. The *Spray* was in the midst of the turbulent Gulf Stream itself. She was jumping around like a porpoise over the uneasy waves.'

He then relates that all was fine until 'Another gale was blowing, accompanied by cross-seas that tumbled about and shook things up with great confusions.' My close-ness to Joshua Slocum helped to banish my long-term fear of electric storms – at least until 0300 hours the next morning.

Lucia and I were sailing under a deep reefed main and a very small amount of jib. I was ten minutes into my rest period, down below, when I jumped in surprise as a huge wave slammed into Lucia's cockpit. At the same moment *Lucia* heeled over at an alarming angle as the winds increased to storm force and she took off like a scalded cat. I grabbed my foul weather jacket and struggled into it as I dashed into the cockpit. Joshua, my wind vane self-steering, was unable to cope.

The next few moments were a flurry of activity. I bent down to release the ropes holding the helm, at the same time trying to clip my harness strap, which was attached to the front of my jacket, to the U-bolt on the cockpit floor. Then I went to the stern to turn off the self-steering. Lightning hit the water with terrifying force, momentarily blinding me. As I struggled with the helm, trying to gain control of *Lucia*, the deafening cracks of thunder struck terror to the roots of my soul. The rain beat viciously at my bare legs, hands and face. As the mountainous waves thundered into the cockpit, I prayed that I would have the strength to endure this storm for as long as it lasted.

Each time I glanced astern to make sure I took the waves on the quarter, hailstones the size of golfballs struck me painfully in the face. To begin with, I thought I must be imagining the size of the hail, but I was not. They were pelting against *Lucia*'s steel coachroof with incredible force. Never in all my life had I seen a storm like this one. When it finally abated, leaving a very lumpy sea, I pointed *Lucia* back on course, reset the self-steering and slumped down in the cockpit, shaking with fatigue.

It was then that I realised my harness strap was not attached to the cockpit U-bolt but hanging useless from the front of my jacket. I thanked the powers that be, for not only giving me the strength to endure but also keeping me safe, when I could so easily have been washed overboard by the huge waves that had flung themselves into the cockpit.

Later I recalled more from Joshua's book, clearly reflecting my own thoughts.

I was at last tired, tired of baffling squalls and fretful cobble-seas. I had not seen a vessel for days and days, where I had expected the company of at least a schooner now and then.

As to the whistling of the wind through the rigging, and the slopping of the sea against the sloop's sides, that was well enough in its way, and we could not have got on without it, the *Spray* and I; but there was so much of it now, and it lasted so long!

In the Gulf Stream, thus late in June, hail stones were pelting the *Spray*, and lightning was pouring down from the clouds, not in flashes alone, but in almost continuous streams.

For the rest of the night I tried to get some rest. When dawn broke I carefully plotted my position; we still had just over two hundred miles to go. Our progress had been very slow, with daily mileages of only sixty to ninety miles. When I eventually went below I wondered what more nature had in store for me. During this passage, due to poor propagation I had had almost no contact with Paul. Knowing that, until he set off on the flight to Boston, he would have been watching the weather very closely, fully aware of the conditions I was experiencing, I hoped he would not be worrying too much about me.

On 17 June darkness descended very early and I wondered what was approaching. Then, over the VHF radio, I heard the coastguard in New York giving out severe weather warnings. My heart sank to an all-time low. Thankfully, all I received was the strobe lights of lightning in the sky as I closed the coast of North America.

During the early hours of the morning, with just thirty miles to go, I could not understand why there was no loom of lights from the land. After all, this was America I was approaching, not some small remote island. As it became lighter I saw ahead of me a wall of fog – the sight of land was completely denied to me. This is yet another situation that strikes me with fear, especially when approaching land. I entertained the illogical hope that it would suddenly rise like a curtain and I would be able to make a safe entry. As we sailed on through the wall of fog the wind died. I started the engine, checked our course on the chart and switched on the electric autopilot.

We continued slowly ahead. Before long, I went forward to drop the mainsail and prepare *Lucia* for harbour. Placing a fender on our portside, I watched in horror as a buoy marking a lobster pot glided past us. Fearful of snagging a rope around the propeller I dashed to the cockpit, took the engine out of gear and went to the bows, praying that this would be an isolated buoy. But as I peered into the dense fog I began to see one after another. I returned to the helm, put *Lucia* in gear and altered course with the aid of the autopilot, carefully steering us round the multitude of lobster pots.

The haunting sound of a distant foghorn added to my already heightened anxiety; the repeated blasts seemed too regular to be another vessel. I studied the chart and identified the horn buoy I could hear. Plotting my position from the GPS, I continued slowly ahead until we had left the sound behind. I repeated this exhausting pattern of navigation as I tried to avoid the unending stream of lobster pots.

Suddenly I heard three blasts of a horn very close to us and responded with a few from my own foghorn. This was followed by the sound of an engine close astern. I gave more blasts and heard the response of the vessel as it passed close by on our portside. The end of this difficult voyage was fast becoming a nightmare. Once again I drew on my inner strength, breathed deeply and told myself that if I just kept my head everything would be fine.

Plotting my position on the chart, I could see that we were close to a small inlet called Mackerel Cove, just to the left of Newport harbour. I decided this would be a safer bet than trying to enter Newport, and carefully inched my way forward. I hoped with all my heart that I could trust my GPS. If it was incorrect, even by a small amount, I risked wrecking *Lucia*.

I heard the sound of breaking surf seconds before I saw it on our portside. I steered Lucia a few degrees to starboard and plotted my position again. We were now entering the cove, and it was imperative that we stay in the centre of the channel. A few minutes later I heard and then saw surf to starboard; I altered course slightly to port. Now I was unable to leave the helm to plot our position, I just had to go by my gut feelings and ease forward until we reached a depth in which to anchor. I saw a shadow on my starboard bow, took Lucia out of gear and held my breath. After a few moments I realised it was a yacht lying to a mooring buoy. I checked my depth, brought *Lucia* to a halt and went forward to drop my anchor.

Unbelievably, the chain jammed in the hawse pipe. Doing my utmost to remain calm, I went below and tried to remove the door to the chain locker. It refused to budge. I rushed to the cutlery drawer, grabbed my large pointed carving knife and prised open the locker door, breaking the tip of the knife in the attempt. Then I released the chain, returned to the bows and successfully lowered the anchor. I went back to the cockpit and motored astern to dig the hook in.

After an extremely tough eight-day passage, *Lucia* and I had finely arrived intact, albeit with every nerve in my body bar-taut. I was desperate for a cup of tea. I went below and, while I waited for the kettle to boil, drank cup after cup of water. Maybe it was the fear that had caused my mouth to get dry – who knows? Whatever, that first cup of tea tasted great. I was halfway through my second when the VHF radio crackled into life.

'*Lucia, Lucia*, this is *Aurora*. Over.'

I sat there in total shock for a moment, then snatched up the radio. '*Aurora*, this is *Lucia*. Over.'

Marijke's voice came back within seconds. 'Sweetheart, where are you?'

'Oh, Marijke, I can't believe it's you. I'm in a little bay called Mackerel Cove. Where are you?'

'We're in Marijke's car in Newport wondering why you're not here to receive the hug I've come all this way to give you.' It was Paul! Immediately I heard his voice the tears began to roll uncontrollably down my face!

'Paul, is that really you?' I sobbed.

'Stay where you are, Mo. We'll make our way to you by road. Thank God you're in. How on earth did you manage it in such dreadful conditions?'

'Well ... surely you've not forgotten I had a very good tutor!'

Very soon another voice called me on the VHF radio; it was the owner of one of the yachts moored in the cove. He lived on top of the hill overlooking the cove and told me that my friends would soon be with me. He had spotted them close to his house, desperately peering through the fog trying to see where I was, and kindly showed them a pathway through his garden that would lead to the beach close to where I was anchored.

By now the fog was lifting slightly and, following this kind stranger's directions, I peered intently in the hope of seeing Paul and Marijke.

'*Lucia*, do you copy? Over.'

'Yes, Paul. Where are you?'

'Waiting on the small beach on your starboard side.'

'Shall I launch the dinghy and come to you?'

'We thought you'd never ask?'

As I made my way to the shore. I could just make out two ghostly figures shrouded in fog. When I stepped on to the beach, their hands reached out to me. As they both embraced me, Paul whispered in my ear.

'Well done, Mo. *Welcome to America*!'

EPILOGUE

I was delighted to keep my promise to the Joshua Slocum Society International. Arriving, as I did, in time for the centenary celebrations, I was given a berth at the Museum of Yachting, Newport, Rhode Island, where Captain Joshua Slocum's amazing voyage around the world is depicted in many photographs and exhibits. The warmth and hospitality of the museum staff, the members of the JSSI and indeed of all the American people whom I met was overwhelming.

After my voyage I was feeling exhausted, and on some days all the attention I was receiving became a little daunting. Paul was an angel during this time. To help me cope with the deluge of questions he printed details of *Lucia*'s voyages and placed them in the museum and in *Lucia*'s windows. Some mornings I would wake to the sound of the voices of people who were looking at *Lucia* and commenting on this or that point concerning my voyages. One day, as I was returning to *Lucia* from a trip into town, I was astounded to be asked for my autograph. By the time I got back on board my face was flushed with embarrassment. Paul thought this was highly amusing!

LONE VOYAGER

On 27 June *Lucia* and I were asked to take part in an opening parade for the celebrations by re-enacting Joshua Slocum's arrival in Newport. At the head of the parade was a replica of the *Spray*, closely followed by *Lucia*, with several other yachts coming up astern. Aboard were my special guests David Sinnett-Jones, Bruce and Gwenda Roberts-Goodson, and of course, Paul. We were given gun salutes as we cruised past the Museum of Yachting and the many yacht clubs in Newport harbour.

At the reception, held in a marquee in the grounds of the International Yacht Restoration School, I was privileged to meet some of Slocum's descendants. Speeches were made and cameras rolled, and I heard my name mentioned many times. Feeling more than a little daunted, I hoped I would not be called upon to speak myself.

I listened intently to the speech given by Isabel Autesia the young Frenchwoman who has sailed single-handed in several around-the-world yacht races, a sailor for whom I had great respect. When she stepped away from the mike after expressing her admiration of single-handed cruising people, I was both delighted and amazed as she walked directly to me and shook my hand. When I was asked to take my turn and relate to the assembled crowd some memories of my voyage, my heart was beating fit to burst. Somehow, with Paul's support I managed to get through the next few moments.

The three days of festivities culminated with a gala centennial dinner and award ceremony. Ted Jones, Commodore of the JSSI, announced the names of those people who were to receive awards and the recipients went up on stage to collect them, after which they gave speeches of thanks. Then Ted announced a Special Recognition Award to Mo Jenkins. With the sound of applause filling the air, my shaky legs just managed to carry me to the stage. June Jones, Secretary and

Treasurer of the JSSI, presented me with a gold pendant replica of the *Spray* for completing my single-handed voyage to Newport via the Azores. I really cannot remember what I said during my speech of thanks because I was so full of emotion. When I returned to my seat, Paul's face was beaming at me as he once again produced his hanky to mop up my tears of joy.

A number of incredible coincidences have come to light, some of which I have mentioned in this book. One that I learnt while in America was that Joshua Slocum had been born on 20 February 1844 in Nova Scotia, Canada. One hundred and fifty years later, on 20 February 1994, *Lucia* was launched. I began my new way of life as he began his, in extremely cold conditions but with my heart filled with a strong desire to endure and enjoy.

During the three years and thirty-one days of my lone voyaging, in the shining light of my life, *Lucia*, I have sailed almost 10,000 miles. I feel that nothing a human being wishes to achieve is out of reach. With determination and the love of like-minded people, I feel anyone can fulfil their dream.

I have found, like many other sailors, that at sea a person's true nature is revealed, especially one's own. I have come to know myself intimately; I have learnt to trust my instincts and act upon them. When the need arose, I have been able to draw on my innermost strengths and resources, no matter how weak my body felt.

I have had that special time, when sailing alone, to examine the parts of my nature I did not like and endeavour to overcome them. I was able to come to terms with the many mistakes I have made in my life, having learnt valuable lessons from them; I felt able to forgive myself. This allowed me to fulfil my desire to obtain peace of mind, along with the bonus of the joy of being at one with my true self.

LONE VOYAGER

I left my beloved *Lucia* on the hard at Wickford ship-yard where, on my return, she would be given a refit in preparation for our next voyage. Shortly afterwards I returned to England to attend the wedding of my son Colin to Giulia, a wonderful person whom I am delighted to have for a daughter-in-law and friend.

My new way of life has surpassed my wildest dreams and given me the confidence and determination to continue to sail alone to the different parts of the world I really want to visit. I will endeavour to carry on, with my hard-fought joy for life, in the spirit of that great master mariner Captain Joshua Slocum and enjoy myself to the full.

GLOSSARY

astro navigation – Method of using the sun and stars to find your position at sea

baby stay – A wire half way up the front of the mast to the fore deck
beam – The width of the boat at the widest part
boom – A spar or tube at the bottom of the mainsail
bowsprit – A pole or tubing that extends the sails past the front of the yacht

cabin sole – A nautical term for the floor
Charlie – The electric autopilot named after the electronics engineer who worked on *Lucia*
coachroof – The part of the cabin raised above the deck

dorade ventilators – Deck-mounted air scoops and attached box to guide ventilation through the yacht

fender – A soft plastic ball or sausage shape used to protect a yacht when alongside a dock
fore stay – A wire from the top of the mast to the front of the yacht or the end of the *bowsprit*

genoa – The largest fore (front) sail

gimbals – Hinges that allow the galley cooker to swing so that pans are not thrown about as the yacht rolls

GPS (Global Positioning System) – An instrument that obtains a yacht's position at sea from data received from a series of satellites

halyard – A rope passing up the mast which is used to raise the sails

hank on sail – The sail that attaches to the *fore stay* or *baby stay* with a series of hooks (hanks)

heads – The toilets

headsail – The sail attached to the *fore stay* also called the head stay

helming by wheel – Steering the yacht by hand with a wheel

hove to – A method of stopping the yacht at sea by turning sideways to the waves and setting the fore sail on the wrong side. The yacht has no forward motion and the wind on the sails steadies the yacht and stops her rolling excessively

jib – Any one of the front sails, for example, *storm jib*, working jib, Yankee jib etc

jib sheet – A rope from the rear corner of the *jib* used to control the set of the sail

Joshua – The *wind vane self-steering* on *Lucia* named after Captain Joshua Slocum, the first man to sail single-handed around the world

line squall – A long line of clouds that have strong winds underneath them

motor sailing – Using both sails and engine together, usually when the wind is light

pulpit – The guard-rail around the front of the yacht and *bowsprit*

reefed mainsail – When the sail area is reduced by partially lowering the sail. Used in strong winds

Samson post – Short bollard or post on the fore deck that the mooring ropes are tied to

sextant – Instrument used to measure the angle between the sun or stars and the horizon to find a position at sea

sheet – Rope used to control the set of a sail

spinnaker – Large sail set on the front of the yacht usually only used in light winds

spreaders – Bars on the mast used to spread the rigging wires

storm jib – Small strong sail set on the *baby stay*, used in strong winds

tacking – Turning the yacht's bow through the wind when sailing into the wind

trade winds – Continuous steady wind found a few degrees north and south of the equator. The name originates from the days before steam when the sailing ships followed them

winds:
    astern – The wind is blowing directly from behind
    gale – 56 kmph (35 mph) upwards
    light wind – between no wind and around 10 mph
    moderate wind – 16 kmph (10 mph) to around 40 kmph (25 mph)
    on the beam – The wind is blowing from the side of the yacht
    on the nose – when the wind is coming from the direction in which you want to go. The yacht must

tack to be able to sail in this direction as it can only sail at around forty-five degrees into the wind

over the quarter – The wind is blowing from behind and to one side

storm force – 113 kmph (70 mph) upwards

strong wind – 40 kmph (25 mph) to around 56 kmph (35 mph)

wind vane self-steering – A mechanical device at the rear of the yacht that senses the direction of the wind and uses this to steer the yacht (nicknamed *Joshua* on *Lucia*)

INDEX

INDEX